Raising the Profile

Whole school maths activities for primary schools

CONTENTS

Introduction   3

Activities
 1. Show a hundred   6
 2. Matchboxes   8
 3. The answer is 6   10
 4. Magic box   12
 5. Crossword   14
 6. What's the question?   16
 7. Which Wally?   18
 8. Nature trail   20
 9. Circle patterns   22
10. Show a half   24
11. Christmas maths   26
12. Magic squares   28
13. Dice and digits   30
14. Partners   34
15. Clown   36
16. Stars   38
17. What a space!   40
18. Pop ups   42
19. Tangram   44
20. Make a box   46
21. Rangoli patterns   48
22. Snail's trails   50
23. Matchstick maths   52
24. Just a minute   54

References and resources   56

INTRODUCTION

WELCOME to what I hope is the first of many such primary resource books to come from the MA publications section. This one has been written partly in response to requests from colleagues and partly because I wanted to help, in some small way, to restore the fun that used to be evident in primary maths. I've chosen to call the book 'Raising the Profile' because that's what I hope it will do – show children (and their families) and the wider school community that maths can be creative and thought provoking and something to talk about with enthusiasm.

Recent UK initiatives have emphasised the open nature of mathematics and the importance of encouraging children to talk about their own strategies or ways of seeing mathematical solutions. The challenges in this book are, if you like, a logical extension of that but with the added freedom to explore, since there is no wrong way of meeting these challenges – only more or less inventive, or sophisticated, or careful. Open-ended activities carefully chosen can use the skills and knowledge that each child, whether young or old, has already mastered. To have the whole school community working and talking for a while about one mathematical topic has unexpected pay-offs, as older children explain to younger ones and parents share the common theme too. You may not choose to use the ideas in that way, but I do suggest that at sometime you give it a try – you may be surprised at the excitement maths can generate.

In school I like to call the ideas 'challenges' but in order to avoid confusion with the M.A. Primary Mathematics Challenge competition, here I refer to them as activities. None of the ideas included here are mind-blowingly original but I hope that in gathering them together and presenting them in one place, you, as hard pressed teachers, maths coordinators or headteachers might be tempted to use them and 'raise the profile' of maths in your school.

INTRODUCTION

THE LAYOUT OF THE BOOK

Each double page spread includes a photocopiable activity page and, on the facing page, ideas for introductions, alternative activities and extension suggestions for younger or older age groups, plus some examples of children's work. At the lower edge of each sheet are brief guidance notes for parents or carers for home based projects.

The activities are grouped according to content, and reference information about resources and the Word files on the accompanying CDrom are on each page. Providing them on disc allows you to adapt or improve them if you wish. There are also some other additional resources listed at the back of the book.

IDEAS FOR USE

Whole school assemblies

Many of these activities were originally devised to be the focus of a monthly whole school assembly. Other curriculum areas had often been the focus of whole school gatherings, but maths was not really considered a suitable topic unless a visiting roadshow or perhaps a competition was involved.

At each assembly I firstly fed back the results from the last activity. I chose children's work from each class (or age group) and asked the children concerned to come to the front, at which point I talked about why I had chosen their work. Sometimes this was to do with an original response, or an extremely carefully produced answer, or perhaps something intentionally amusing. As a staff we were often surprised by the time, and energy, expended by children who perhaps did not particularly shine in the daily maths lesson. It was an opportunity for the younger children to see what the older pupils had done, and increased the understanding that there may be many possible responses to a problem. The children who were chosen were presented with a 'maths challenge' pencil and their work, together with a selection of other pupils' work, was awarded a sticker and used in the display in the entrance hall of the school.

INTRODUCTION

In introducing the next challenge I tried to vary the content so that a number-based challenge would be followed by a shape and space or measure challenge, and so on. From the children I drew several examples of the sort of response I was expecting to get, leaving some unanswered questions to provide extra challenge for the older or more able children. Entry to the challenge was voluntary and we stressed the importance of just 'having a go'. Some of the parents took this as on open invitation to submit their own responses too, and on occasions we had entries from non-teaching and kitchen staff, and governors, who duly received pencils and had their work displayed (if it reached an appropriate standard!).

Maths clubs

You may choose to use the activities in a maths club. Because the challenges are open-ended they lend themselves to co-operative work and the children often complete one challenge and then, having seen how others respond, choose to repeat the challenge because they have had a better idea.

Choosing time

Another possibility might be to have the sheets available as choosing time options in your classroom, as on-going activities for children who have finished their work. You might choose to link the challenge with the topic being studied in the daily maths lesson, or offer something totally different as light relief.

Take home sheets

It's good to be able to send something home which is intended to be a fun, shared activity. Parents and carers often respond very positively to maths activities which they can't get wrong....

Post Script

You could raise the profile of maths in your school even higher! Why not send outstanding examples of children's responses to Primary Mathematics for publication? Or suggest that the children make up their own challenges ……….and submit those for others to use?

Lynne McClure

Show a hundred.........................A pattern, a picture, a sum, a model........you choose.

Name: _____ Class: _____

My title: _____

Help for grown-ups:
The solution may perhaps involve collecting 100 small objects such as buttons or pennies, drawing, making a 3-d model, or making up a very difficult sum. Your child may realise that there are many possible different arrangements for a hundred - encourage exploration!

Date back to school: _____

Show a hundred

Introductions

For younger children a hundred is a very big number and they may need help in counting accurately. As an introduction you may wish to show a linear display such as 100 pieces of pasta threaded on a string, or a pattern illustrating an array of 10 x 10 items, or perhaps for older pupils a shape with an area of 100cm², or a complicated calculation, the answer to which is 100.

Extensions/alternatives

You could:
- use for the 100th day of school, for a 100th anniversary or when 100 is in the news
- change the number to 1000 for older children. Or even a million …..
- whilst the young ones are focusing on the magnitude of a hundred, the older ones could be encouraged to make a display of different ways of representing say, a hundred dots.

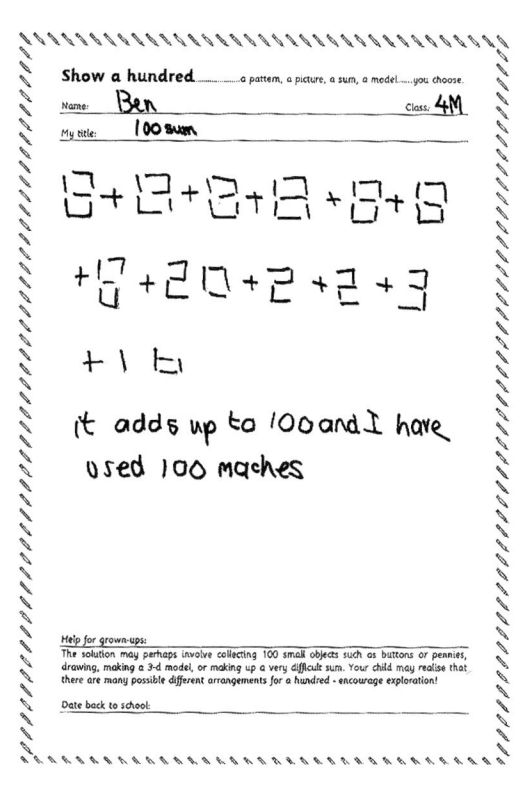

Resources: Show a hundred
10² book and poster ATM

Matchboxes

How many *different* items can you get inside a matchbox?

Name _____ Class: _____

Here's my list.... _____

I fitted ☐ things into my matchbox

Help for grown-ups:
Finding very small items can be fascinating. If you have a magnifying glass you can have a lot of fun looking at the detail of natural items such as a human hair, the stamen of a flower, or a (dead) insect!

Date back to school: _____

Matchboxes

Introductions

The idea behind this activity is to introduce, or remind, or reinforce, the idea of awe and wonder in maths. You could introduce the idea by asking the children what is the smallest thing they could hold in their hand. If you have a microscope which can be used in a whole school setting, you could illustrate the structure of a couple of prearranged items. The 'power of ten' website has a superb series of photographs starting with a view of earth from outer space and getting closer and more highly magnified up to the cell structure of an insect.

Extensions/alternatives

You could:

- make a display of photographs or pictures of magnified objects – perhaps with a quiz asking what they represent
- with older children, talk about estimating sensibly and calculate how many of something very small are in something of a reasonable size – how many grains of rice in a teaspoon for example
- talk about how we record very small measurements. How can we work out how thick a piece of paper is even though it is too thin to measure?

Resources: Matchbox
Website, powers of ten.

The answer is 6. ...

Your questions could use pictures, different kinds of sums, or even models.

Name _____   Class: _____

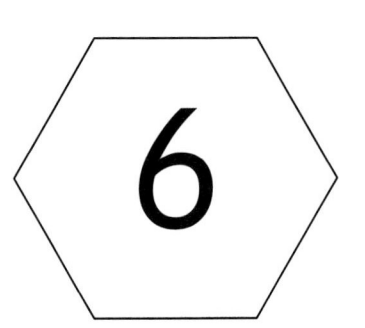

⬡ 6

Help for grown-ups:
Encourage your child to brainstorm as many different ways of making the number as possible before filling up the sheet. You may want to do this over several days, as more ideas will undoubtedly come to you both as you notice more instances of 6 around. Don't be constrained by the space on the sheet – be creative!!

Date back to school: _____

The answer is 6.

Introductions

How to introduce the number six? I've done this by bringing objects or pictures out of a 'magic box', and asking the children what it is that they all have in common. Six occurs in nature frequently so you may get some natural artefacts brought to school as examples if you include one or two in your collection.

Or ask the early years children to come to the front and tell the 'story of six'. You could start with six balloons, for example, and distribute them differently to illustrate the number bonds.

Or play the clapping game – ask the whole group to count 1,2,3,4 etc. out loud and clap all the even numbers, up to about 30 or so. Even the little ones will be able to join in. Then ask the older children to clap the three times table. Then get both groups to clap together and ask what they notice. Hopefully some will volunteer that there are some numbers that everyone claps – and that these are the six times table. All these are good ways in to what makes a number special.

Extensions/alternatives

You could:
- challenge older children to use compasses to draw a hexagon inside a circle and look for patterns of six in repeats of different shapes
- challenge the children to make different arrangements of six shapes – hexagons or squares, or triangles
- use a digital camera to take photos of occurrences of six in nature, to make a display
- did you know six is the first perfect number? That's because the sum of its factors is the number itself, 1 + 2 + 3 = 6. You could investigate factors and find the next perfect number, and the next…

Resources: The answer is 6
 Numbers fact figures and fiction

Magic box

What's your rule? Perhaps everything comes out twice as big ...or half the size.. or upside down......or matching..........show some ins and outs for others to guess your rule.

Name: _____ Class: _____

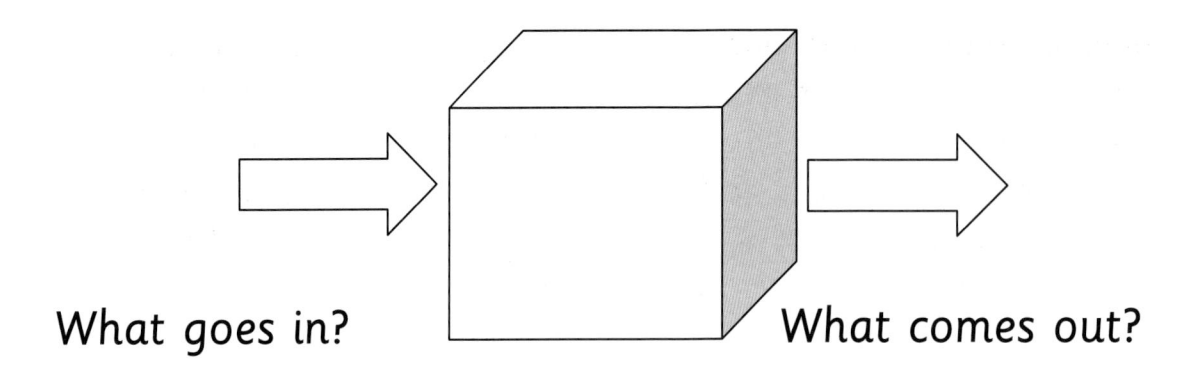

What goes in? → ☐ → What comes out?

Guess my rule!!! (it's on the back)

Help for grown-ups:
You could choose to make this either a number or shape activity. The magic box has to do the same to each number put in, so if the rule is add 2, then 5 becomes 7, 100 becomes 102 etc. If a shape is put in, it will be changed in some way – made wider, or twice as tall, or turned around..........

Date back to school: _____

Magic box

Introductions

I often use a magic box as a way of attracting the children's attention. In this case it's being used as a function machine, and the objective is for the children to see that although different things come out, the rule stays the same. For the younger pupils you could bring out the partner – eg knife goes in, fork comes out, or a number goes in and is doubled (I like to use objects rather than numerals to make the point), or a subtle one is to put in a picture of a 2-d shape and bring out one which has one less side. Sneaky!

Extensions/alternatives

You could:
- read the story 'Anno's mysterious multiplying jar' to emphasise the power of doubling
- make a display with the magic box and a different rule for ins and outs each day
- use the box backwards – what went in if ………came out?
- check out the primary strategy website and download the function machine interactive resource, and counter.

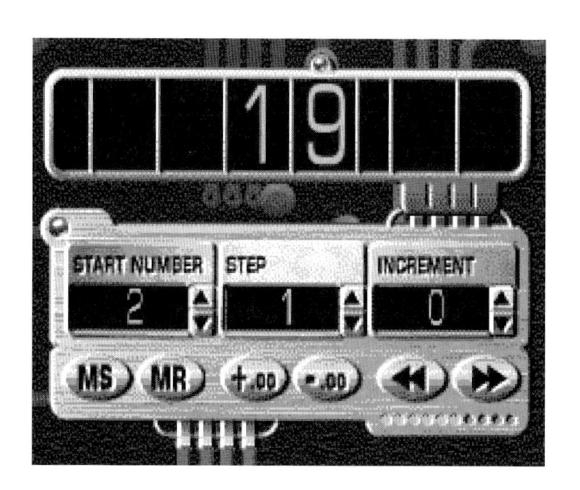

Resources: ■ Magic box
      📖 Anno's mysterious multiplying jar
      🖱 NNS counting machine, function machine

Crossword ...... Make up your own crossword then write the clues.

Name: _____   Class: _____

Clues
Across   Down
1.

Help for grown-ups:
You might want to start by listing mathematical words, and, if you have a Scrabble set, using the letters to help you to work out how to fit them together. Number the beginning letter of each word and work out the clues. Draw the empty crossword and clues on this side, and draw the solution on the back.

Date back to school:

Crossword

Introductions

The intention in this activity is to focus more on the accuracy of the clues than the fitting of the words together. You could introduce the activity by displaying your own crossword and clues (for a short cut go to www.edhelper.com/crossword.htm where you can enter answers and clues and the crossword will be generated) and asking for answers from the children. Then put up a blank grid and go through the process of filling in intersecting words, and writing clues for them.

Extensions/alternatives

You could:

- make a display of crosswords to illustrate the rotational symmetry and suggest that older pupils create crosswords that use this element of design
- for older children restrict the content to a specific topic eg: shape
- change the crossword to a cross number
- play the Fourbidden card game – one team guesses the target word as the other describes it without using the four words on the card.

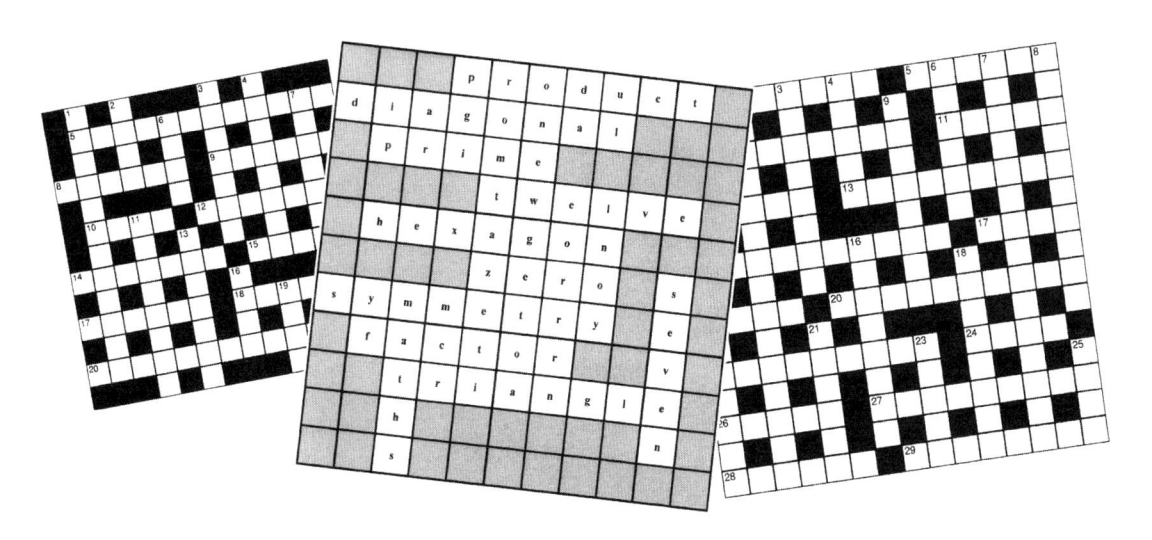

Resources: Crossword
 Hangman, cross number and cross word websites
R Fourbidden card game

What's the question?......

What's your favourite number? Write it in the sun and make up some interesting questions to write in the clouds.

Name _____   Class: _____

Help for grown-ups:
What's your child's favourite number? You may wish to think about this for a few days before filling in the clouds.

Date back to school: _____

What's the question?:

Introductions

The ultimate in the open ended question!! You could introduce this challenge by sharing your favourite number with the children, and perhaps asking some of your colleagues to share theirs too. A range of questions involving arithmetical calculation, shape, and general knowledge facts makes an interesting mix. The Richard Phillips book takes numbers up to a million and gives fascinating facts about each which can be used as a starter.

Extensions/alternatives

You could:
- ask a particular class or group of children to debate the merits or otherwise of choosing particular numbers
- have two different numbers which are connected in some way, such as 5 and 10 and use the results to start a huge version of this in a public place such as the entrance hall and encourage anyone and everyone to add their suggestions
- restrict the sort of questions for different year groups – year five and six aren't allowed addition or subtraction, years four and three must include at least one fraction in their questions, etc.
- suggest that the favourite number could be other than a whole one.

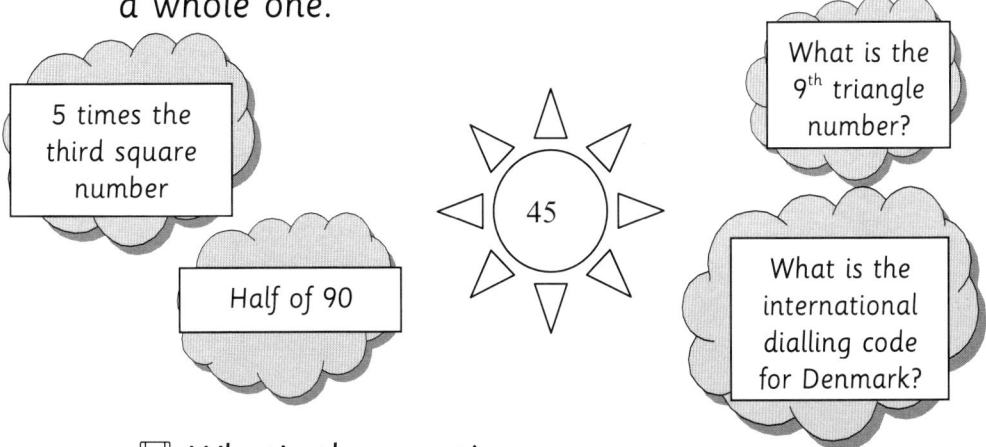

> 5 times the third square number
>
> Half of 90
>
> 45
>
> What is the 9th triangle number?
>
> What is the international dialling code for Denmark?

Resources: What's the question
Numbers fact figures and fiction

Which Wally?........

How many different Wallys can you make? How do you know if you've got them all?

Name _____ Class: _____

I made _____ different Wallys

Wally always wears one of his four hats. Draw them here:

[ ]   [ ]   [ ]   [ ]

Sometimes he wears his scarf or bow tie. Draw them here:

[ ]   [ ]

He always wears one of his two jackets:

[ ]   [ ]

He's only got one pair of trousers, so he always wears those:

[ ]

And he's got two pairs of shoes to choose from

[ ]   [ ]

Draw all the different outfits Wally could dress up in.

Help for grown-ups:
You could do this randomly or, with older children help them to work systematically. Use different colours to help.

Date back to school: _____

Which Wally?

Introductions

This is a good activity to include some of the younger children. If you can have the clothes in a basket you can dress the children up to give an idea of the combinations that are possible. The sheet is a little sneaky in that it says that Wally SOMETIMES wears a scarf or bow tie – older pupils might realise that there is a no neckwear option too!

Extensions/alternatives

You could:

- support the younger children by giving a photocopy page of undressed Wallys (see disc)
- ask the children to make up their own questions like this and make a display of them with answers – older children will realise that there is a underlying similar structure to obtaining the complete solution set. In this example, there are 4x2x2x1x2=32 different Wallys, or 4x2x3x1x2 if you count no neckwear as an option
- look for activities that require systematic organisation of all combinations such as those on the 'nrich' website
- have an interactive display in the entrance hall where teddies can be dressed in a variety of different clothes. If you make some blank teddy cards on the disc, the children can record the outfits and you can then sort them in all sorts of ways. I find that's a good way to talk about the activity when everyone has had a go.

Resources: Which Wally
 nrich

Nature trail

Do all flowers have the same number of petals? Do all ladybirds have the same number of spots? Do some numbers pop up in nature more often than others? Can you find an example of each number somewhere around you?

Name: _____ Class: _____

1

2

3

4

5

6

7

8

9

10

11

12

20

☐ is also an interesting number because

Help for grown-ups:
Older children might just want to record their findings while younger ones may wish to draw their discoveries. Try to encourage them to find examples which are always true — for example, all spiders have eight legs.

Date back to school: _____

Nature trail

Introductions

Some numbers do pop up in nature more often than others, notably Fibonacci numbers (1,2,3,5,8 etc). You could introduce the activity by bringing in a collection of flowers or pictures of insects or animals and counting the petals or legs or wings………did you know that all members of the rose family show five-fold symmetry in their fruits and flowers, whereas flowers with a three-fold symmetry are likely to be grown from bulbs? With younger children you could start with the numbers of body parts. Did you know that infants have 20 teeth whilst adults usually have 32?

Extensions/alternatives

You could:
- make a large display of the numbers to 20 and other exceptional ones, and encourage children to add to it by bringing photographs, their own drawings, or real objects
- make a display of body maths. You could include the numbers of bones, chromosomes, or the relationship between the lengths of different parts of the body such as those discovered by Leonardo da Vinci.

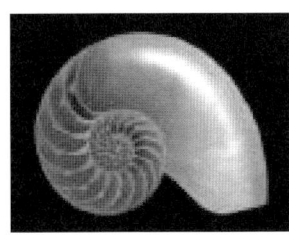

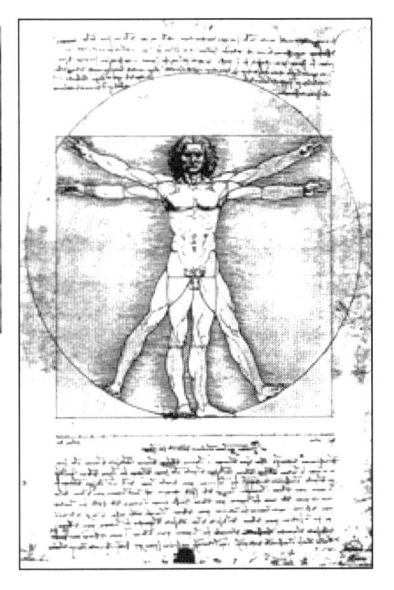

Resources: Nature trail
 Thinkquest

Circle patterns

............Number the points, then think of a rule and join up the points to make a pattern.

Name: _____   Class: _____

My rule is: _____

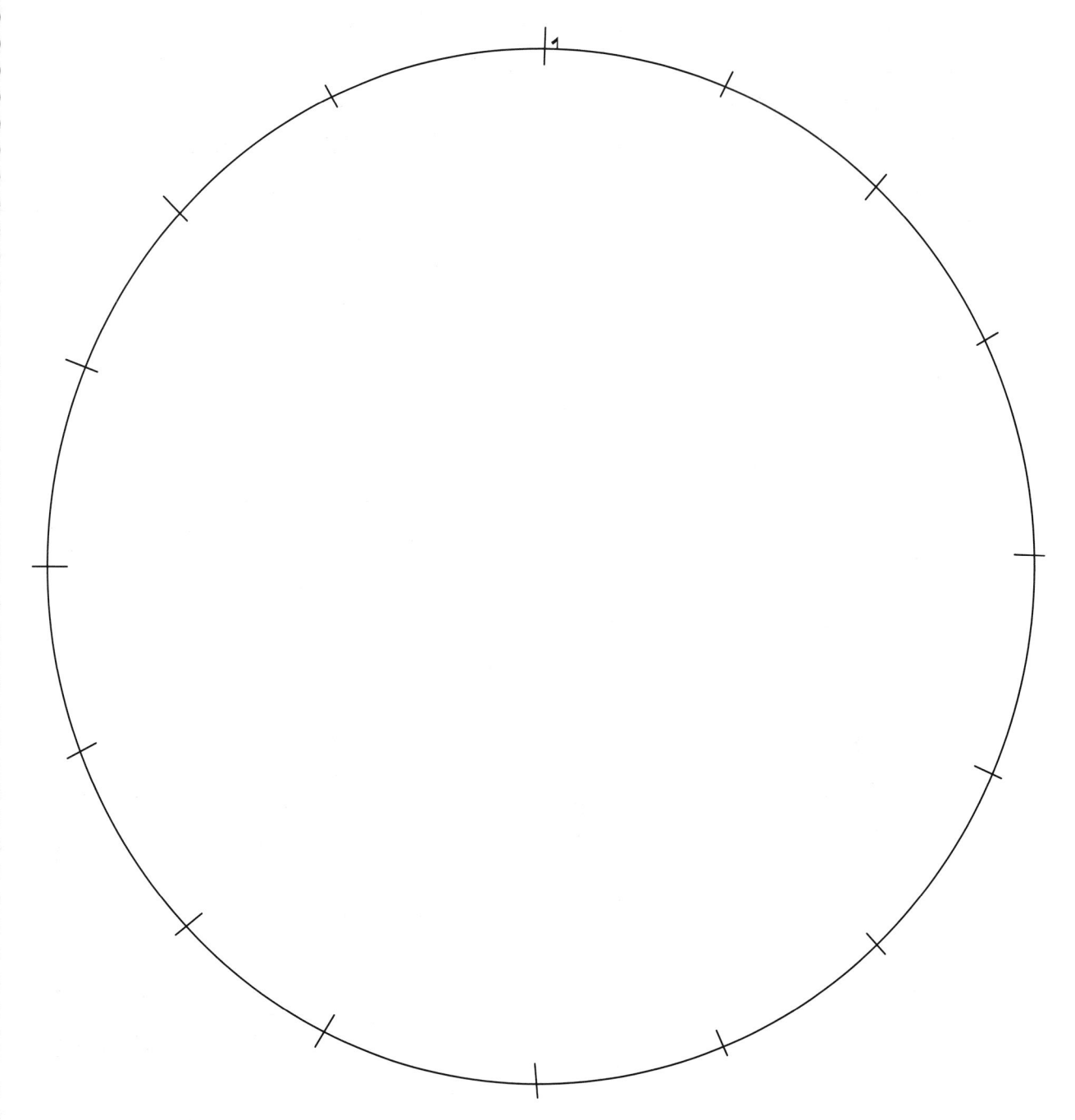

1

Help for grown-ups:
Number the dots in order. Think of a rule, for example add two, and join them up in order, 1-3-5-7 to make a pattern. You might want to suggest continuing the numbering round the circle more than once, or your child may want to add extra dots and renumber them. Colouring will emphasise the pattern too.

Date back to school: _____

Circle patterns

Introductions

This particular challenge links the visual with the numerical – a very powerful way of helping some children to make the connections in number patterns. A selection of pictures where the rule is to add a constant (add one, add two etc) produces a regular pattern with different numbers of points in a star and a different sized hole in the middle. Introducing the idea of multiplication emphasises the fact that the numbers get larger. If you have a circular perspex pinboard then you can model this on an OHP, otherwise prepare a transparency of the sheet and try a couple of different rules. Asking for predictions of the pattern and a justification for the prediction can produce some interesting explanations.

Extensions/alternatives

You could:

- use numbered children standing in a circle, and a ball of string passed between them according to a rule. If you hold the string up high in the air and then at the end lay the pattern on the floor, you will be surprised at the gasps of amazement!
- use the 'nrich' website to investigate star patterns
- for older children suggest that they investigate the different patterns in a systematic way, perhaps as a group.

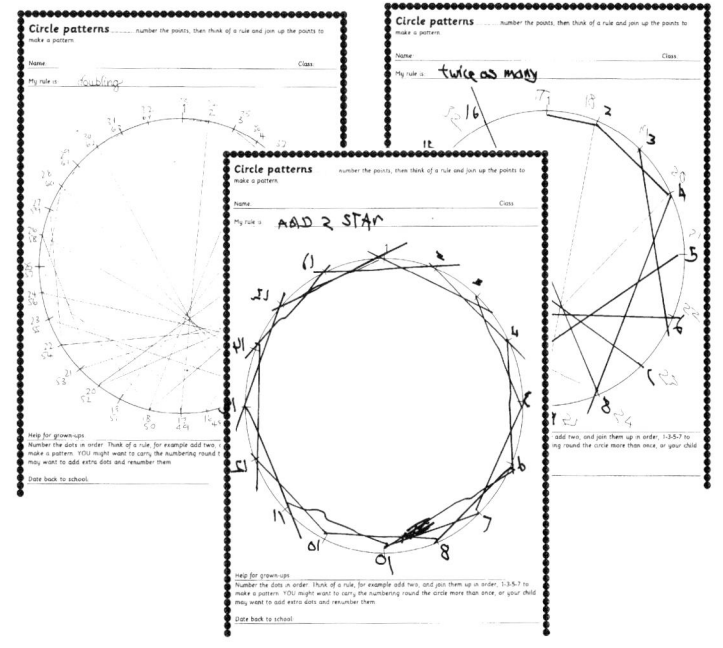

Resources: Circle patterns
nrich website

Show a half

Name: _____   Class: _____

My title: _____

Help for grown-ups

Younger children may well fill in the left or right hand side with a pattern. Older children may even subdivide the squares into smaller parts. Whichever, they need to cover in the equivalent of 50 squares.

Date back to school: _____

Show a half

Introductions
The mesmeric Smile programme 'Take Half' has been updated and placed on the NNS website as a downloadable programme, 'Take part'. It makes a wonderful introduction to the spatial idea of a half. Failing that, you could use an OHP and a transparency of the hundred grid to elicit ideas from the children. Some of course will take it literally…..see below.

Extensions/alternatives
You could:
- use a different fraction – perhaps a quarter – although to make it inclusive for the little ones you'll need to make sure it's not more difficult than that
- change the number of squares in the grid
- change the grid and make it a circular cake or pizza with lots of slices, or a subdivided triangle…or…(see below)
- choose to have no guidance as to shape – but you will need to do a very clear introduction in that case.

Resources: 💾 Show a half

Christmas maths

There were more presents each day. How many altogether? Show how you found out.

Name: _____   Class: _____

I think there are _____ presents altogether

On the twelfth day of Christmas..
  12 pipers piping
  11 drummers drumming
  10 lords a-leaping
  9 ladies dancing
  8 maids a-milking
  7 swans a-swimming
  6 geese a-laying
  5 gold rings
  4 calling birds
  3 French hens
  2 turtle doves
and a partridge in a pear tree

Help for grown-ups:
There are many different ways of working out the number of presents altogether. The obvious one is to write out each days' total and add them all up – perhaps using a calculator. If your child is a little older, you could together look for different patterns and a quicker way to do the calculation.

Date back to school: _____

Christmas maths

Introductions

I like to introduce this by inviting children out to the front. I have pictures of the various presents so as we recite the poem I ask the first child to hold up a picture of a partridge in a pear tree. For the 2nd day two children come out, one to hold another partridge and one to show two turtle doves. I build this up until about day 5. Without an indication about the start of the pattern many children just add up the present total for day 12 rather than realising they have to add day 1 and day 2 and day 3 etc. to get a total. If you are more musically adept you may wish to suggest that your colleagues perform the song, with actions, and leave it at that...

Extensions/alternatives

You could:

- with older pupils help them to look for a pattern and generalise to more days
- work out what would happen to the pattern if, on day one, there were 12 partridges, on day two 12 partridges and eleven turtle doves etc. Does the total work out the same?
- play 'my aunt went shopping' and alter the number of items each day to be an even number.....my aunt went shopping and she bought 2 buns..... my aunt went shopping and she bought 2 buns and 4 bananas....... my aunt went shopping and she bought 2 buns and 4 bananas and 6 apples - what happens to the patterns?

Note – the answer is 364 – 12x1, 11x2, 10x3, 9x4, 8x5, 7x6, 6x7, 5x8, 4x9, 3x10, 2x11, 1x12, or (12x1, 11x2, 10x3, 9x4, 8x5, 7x6) x2

Resources: Christmas maths
                The twelve days of Christmas

Magic squares .....

Put the numbers 1,2,3,4,5,6,7,8,9 anywhere you like.
See what patterns you can find........

Name: Class:

These are my patterns

Help for grown-ups:
Cut out pieces of paper or card with the numbers 1-9. Explore what sorts of patterns you can make – for example can you put the numbers so that each row adds up to an even number? Or an odd number? Or the same number? There are endless possibilities. Record the most interesting array above and note down the patterns.

Date back to school:

Magic squares

Introductions

Another very open ended question which can produce all sorts of interesting answers. The typical magic square is of course the one where each row, column and diagonal adds to the same number – for numbers 1-9 this would be 15 with 5 in the middle square (why?). But I introduce this by putting the numbers in order and asking what patterns anybody notices. In this case the sums of each row, column and diagonal add up to a multiple of 3. This encourages the children to look for other ways of entering the numbers – usually the older ones have seen the original magic square so this gives them an opportunity to be more creative.

1	4	7
2	5	8
3	6	9

Extensions/alternatives

You could:
- tell the Chinese story of Lo Shu, the divine turtle with a magic square on his shell
- ask the children how many solutions to the 3x3 magic square there are and how they relate to each other (through rotational and reflective symmetry)
- set up a display with a 4x4 grid and Velcro backed numbers 1-16
- explore the history of magic squares across different nations
- explore one of the magic square websites for interactive activities.

Resources: Magic squares
   Lo Shu math forum website
   magic squares website

Dice and digits: make a game

Introductions

My favourite resource is a box of dice – all sorts and shapes, including 1-6 cubes and blank ones. The following activities although having a common objective, are at three different levels for different ages or abilities of children. The simpler grid is the one I give to KS 1 children and their parents as 0-99 is just too difficult – however if you offer a free choice it can be interesting to see which the children pick.

The one which produced the most talk was the 0-99 grid as the children tried to work out which were the good numbers and which were the awkward ones - either difficult or impossible to make using two 1-6 dice.

The blank grid is interesting as there is a lot of arithmetic and underlying probability theory underlying decisions about which numbers to put on the grid and where.

Extensions/alternatives

You could:

- choose the best and, once you are sure they worked, decorate them, laminate them and keep them for choosing time at playtime and wet play
- use the blank grid as a data handling exercise. Everyone in the class throws the two dice and records the number of times each of the different scores is made by whatever rule is being used (adding, multiplying, squaring etc). Some scores occur often – why? Some never occur – why? Then choose suitable numbers based on the classes findings, to fill in the grid.

Resources: Dice and digits 1,2,3

Dice and digits 1
Use the board and one or two dice, or a spinner. You may want to use buttons for counters too. Write the rules of your game on the back.

Name: _____ Class: _____

Name of my game: _____

0	1	2	3	4	5	6	7	8	9
10	11	12	13	14	15	16	17	18	19
20	21	22	23	24	25	26	27	28	29
30	31	32	33	34	35	36	37	38	39
40	41	42	43	44	45	46	47	48	49
50	51	52	53	54	55	56	57	58	59
60	61	62	63	64	65	66	67	68	69
70	71	72	73	74	75	76	77	78	79
80	81	82	83	84	85	86	87	88	89
90	91	92	93	94	95	96	97	98	99

Help for grownups:

If you've got dice at home, you could use the number of spots to decide which numbers to cover, perhaps by multiplying, or adding, or squaring....   If you don't have dice you could make spinners from card board circles and matchsticks.
Choose the rule for covering the numbers on the grid.
Say what you have to do to win (for example cover three in a row).
Playing the game several times will help to iron out any unfairness or problems.

Date back to school:

Dice and digits 2:
Use the board and one or two dice, or a spinner. You may want to use buttons for counters too. Write the rules of your game on the back.

Name: _____   Class: _____

Name of my game: _____

1	7	3	8	5	10
6	8	2	9	4	11
5	9	1	10	3	12
4	10	6	11	2	7
3	11	5	12	1	8
2	12	4	7	6	9

Help for grown-ups:
If you don't have dice you could make a spinner from a card board circle and a matchstick. Playing the game several times will help to iron out any unfairness or problems.

Choose your dice or spinners.
Choose the rule for covering the numbers on the grid (for example, add the dots).
Say what you have to do to win (for example cover three in a row).

Date back to school: _____

Dice and digits 3:
Use the board and one or two dice, or a spinner. You may want to use buttons for counters too. Write the rules of your game on the back.

Name: _____   Class: _____

Name of my game: _____

Help for grown-ups:
If you don't have dice you could make a spinner from a card board circle and a matchstick. Playing the game several times will help to iron out any unfairness or problems, and may help to choose more suitable numbers for the grid.

Choose your dice or spinners.
Choose the numbers to put on the grid (you might want to use pencil until you are sure).
Choose the rule for covering the numbers on the grid (for example, add the dots).
Say what you have to do to win (for example cover three in a row).

Date back to school: _____

Partners

Choose pairs of numbers from the ones below and say why they make good partners

Name: _____ Class: _____

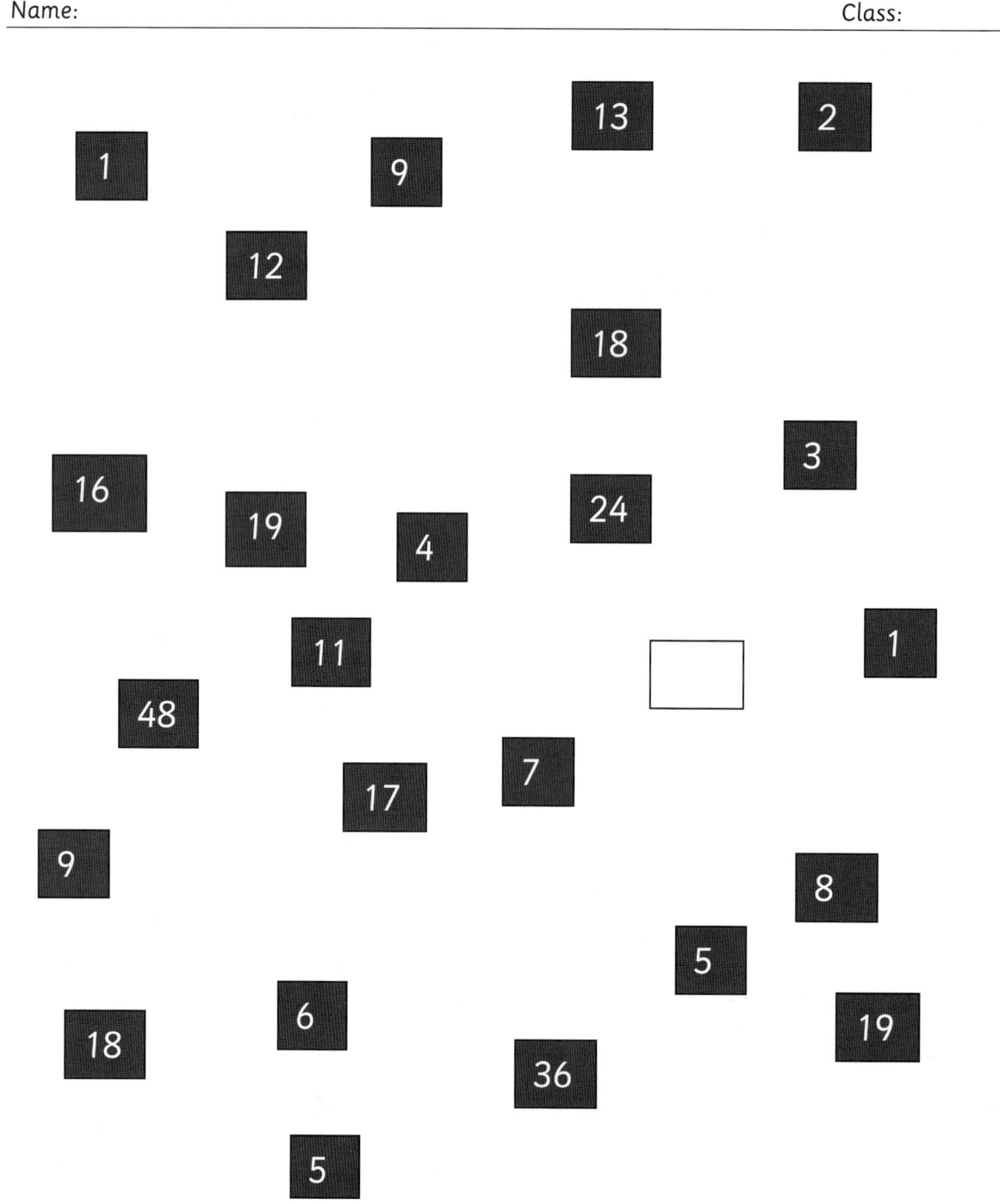

1   9   13   2
12
18
16   3
   19   4   24
            1
   11
48
      17   7
9
         8
         5
18   6   19
         36
   5

Help for grown-ups:

There are lots of possibilities here – there may be one reason to connect lots of different pairs (they add up to a certain number for example) or your child may find lots of different reasons for connecting two numbers. There's no right or wrong – the reason just needs to be stated. You might want to use a coloured pencil to join the numbers and write the reason along the line. There's a space for you to add one of your own too. Can you use them all up?

Date back to school: _____

Partners

Introductions

I introduce this by telling the story of ten, much as the introduction to the 'The answer is 6' activity. Then we discuss the idea of partners and how numbers can be connected by adding or multiplying, or some other type of connection. I put up an OHT with a selection of different numbers and ask the children to suggest partners and why. It's an excuse to look at number bonds, but the older children will find lots of other possibilities too.

Extensions/alternatives

You could:
- ask the children to make up their own sets of partners according to a certain rule and give them to a friend as a challenge
- link this activity to the counter or function machine activities in the 'magic box' activity
- investigate target numbers rich in factors such as 36 and see how many multiplication partners can be found in an ordered way.

Resources: Partners

Clown

Make both sides match. You could add a hat, or a bow tie, too!

Name: _____ Class: _____

Name of my clown: _____

Help for grown-ups:
This could be done by drawing, or painting, or perhaps by making a collage. To make the face symmetrical, you could cut out shapes from a folded piece of paper, and stick one on each side of the centre line so that both sides match. Older pupils could use ruler and compasses to construct and measure accurately. You could use a real mirror to check!

Date back to school:

Clown

Introductions

Symmetry is fascinating to most children. You could introduce this activity through the 'magic mirror' where a child has to copy exactly what you do. Or cut a set of dancing dolls from a concertina of paper to show how both sides match. Or produce examples from nature in which line symmetry is evident. From older children you could tease out what exactly they mean by 'matching' and draw out the idea of object and image (corresponding shapes) being the same distance away from the mirror line. Or if you are really daring take some face paints and draw a symmetrical pattern on the face of a child ……..or a colleague..

Extensions/alternatives

You could:
- challenge the children to bring in symmetrical faces or other pictures to supplement a whole school display
- use half faces in art so that the children have to complete the face
- use a digital camera to take photos of the children and, by reflecting each half in turn, show that we would look slightly strange if we were symmetrical
- suggest that older children use more sophisticated drawing equipment eg rulers and compasses to ensure accuracy.

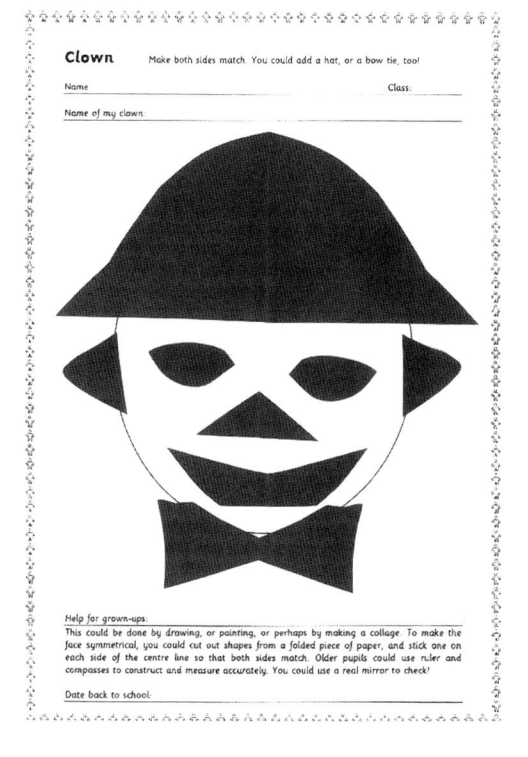

Resources: Clown

Stars

What is a star? You could draw one here, or make a model of one as part of our display.

Name: _____   Class: _____

Help for grown-ups:
Try to tease out your child's understanding of a star. Young children may draw them freehand, but you could encourage them to try to make all the points the same...or different...or make a 3-d star from straws.........the possibilities are endless!

Date back to school _____

Stars

Introductions

I have often used this as our Christmas assembly as the resulting products make a very festive display. I begin by asking for a description of a star, and once several children have had a go we make a communal agreement – usually something like ' a centre bit with lots of points coming off it'. Not very scientific or mathematical but enough to get us started. I then show them some pictures of fantastic stars - both 2-d and 3-d and suggest that a judicious use of glitter might enhance the end products.

Extensions/alternatives

You could:

- make links to the Circle pattern activity and encourage star production within a circle. How do we make sure the points are equally spaced? Is it possible to draw stars by connecting the points on the circumference of a circle in a continuous line?
- suggest that older children use more sophisticated drawing equipment eg rulers and compasses to ensure accuracy
- investigate some of the mathematical models of stellated polyhedra and perhaps make them as a class project
- try out some of the wonderful folded tissue paper window stars from the Tarquin publication – they make a stunning classroom decoration.

Resources: Stars
 Robert Webb
 Kaleidometrics
 Altair grids

Reproduced with permission from Robert Webb

What a space! .... What can you make with 20 squares? Cut them out and make a picture. Give it a name.

Name: _____ Class: _____

Name of my picture: _____

What is the l o n g e s t shape you can make?
What is the w i g g l i e s t shape you can make?
What is the most interesting shape you can make?

Help for grown-ups:
The picture could be made with whole squares, or the squares can be cut up to make other shapes. But all of every square must be used!

Date back to school: _____

What a space!

Introductions

The idea of conservation of area is a sophisticated one. In this activity I like to start by showing a couple of 2-d shapes which have the same area and asking what's the same about them. Then I rearrange the first shape into the other and we talk about the area or the space they take up being the same.

Extensions/alternatives

You could:
- ask for the shape with the longest perimeter......shortest perimeter
- suggest that the shape should be symmetrical – either line or rotational symmetry
- have look at the investigations about area on the 'nrich' website. The GRRRRRREAT SQUARES one has lots of open ended questions for older children.

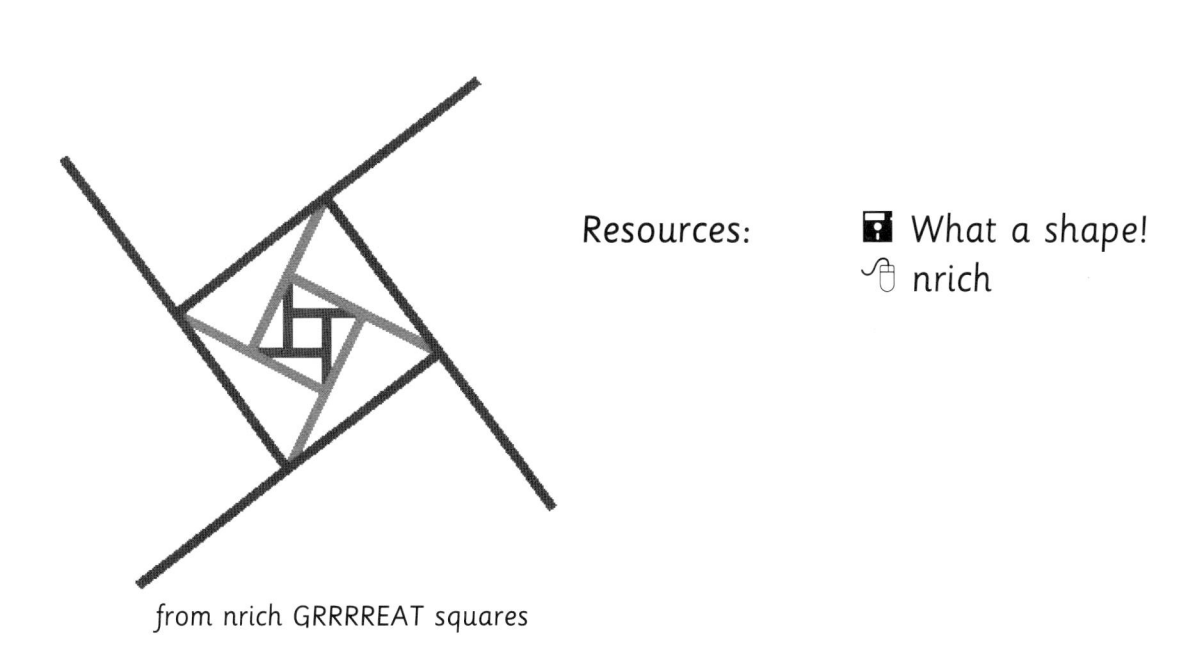

Resources: What a shape!
             nrich

from nrich GRRRREAT squares

Pop-ups .... Surprise a friend by making a pop-up card.

Name: _____   Class: _____

My card is for: _____

Instructions

1. Take two identical pieces of paper and fold them in half.

2. On one of the pieces, cut a line into the fold

3. Fold the flaps back to make triangles

4. Open the flaps and then open up the paper

5. Push the triangle through from the outside to the inside to make a mouth

6. Make a picture using the mouth then glue the other piece of paper onto the outside

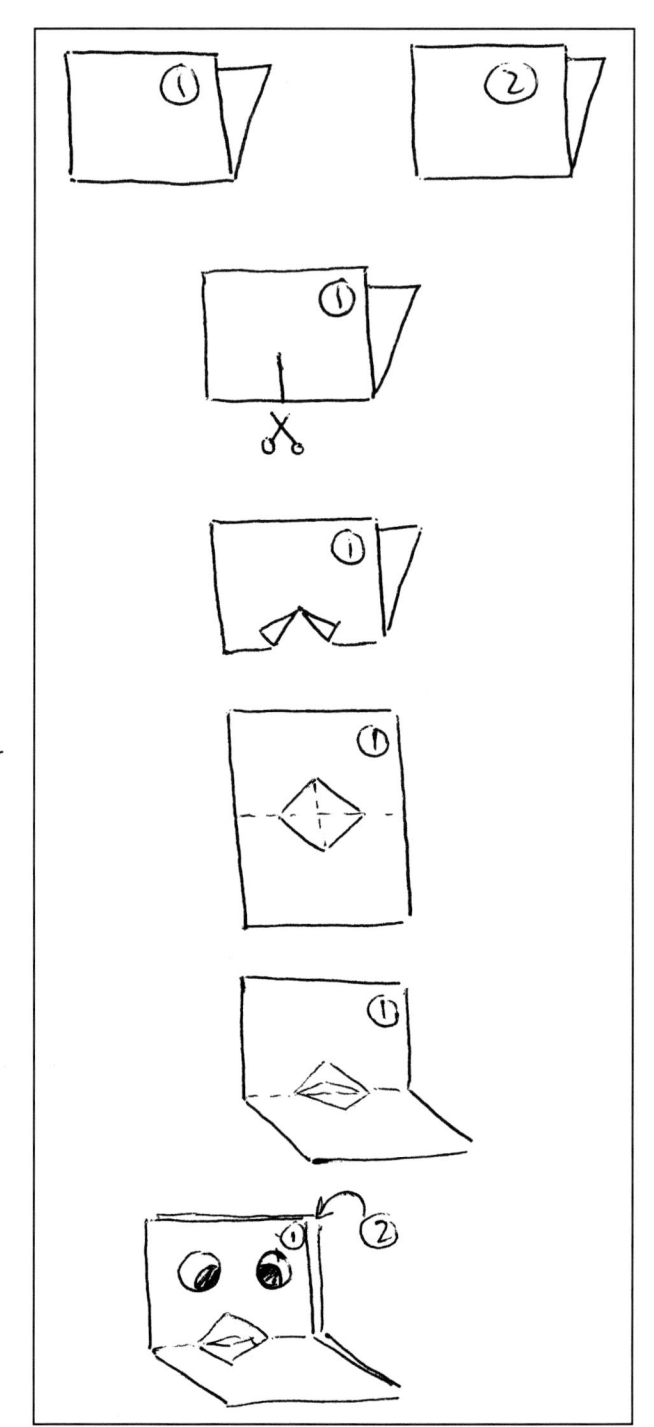

Help for grown-ups:
If your child is young, you may need to help with the mechanics the first time, but do let them have go by themselves. Older children might like to try making more than one flap, or different sized flaps, or different shaped flaps…..

Date back to school: _____

Pop-ups

Introductions

If you have collection of pop - up cards then showing them to the children can be a good enough introduction. The one on the sheet is a simple mouth flap, but if you have them you can take apart more mathematical ones that use rectangular steps onto which pop-up shapes can be stuck.

Extensions/alternatives

You could:
- make a display of the various cards
- suggest that older children have to have more than one flap
- investigate how you make a flap on top of a flap –

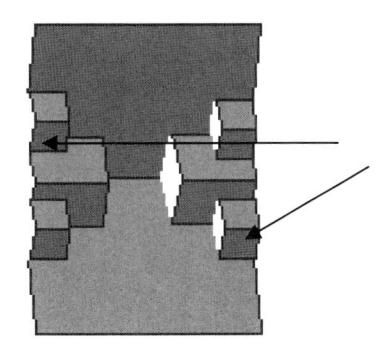

cut out rectangular flaps and stick shapes onto the front of them

- expect more sophisticated and accurate examples from the older children
- support younger children by using squared paper for the inside sheet of paper.

Resources: Pop-ups
             Fractal cuts
             Robert Sabuda

from Robert Sabuda website

Tangram

Cut out the pieces and make a picture which uses all of them. Give your picture a name.

Name: _____ Class: _____

My picture is: _____

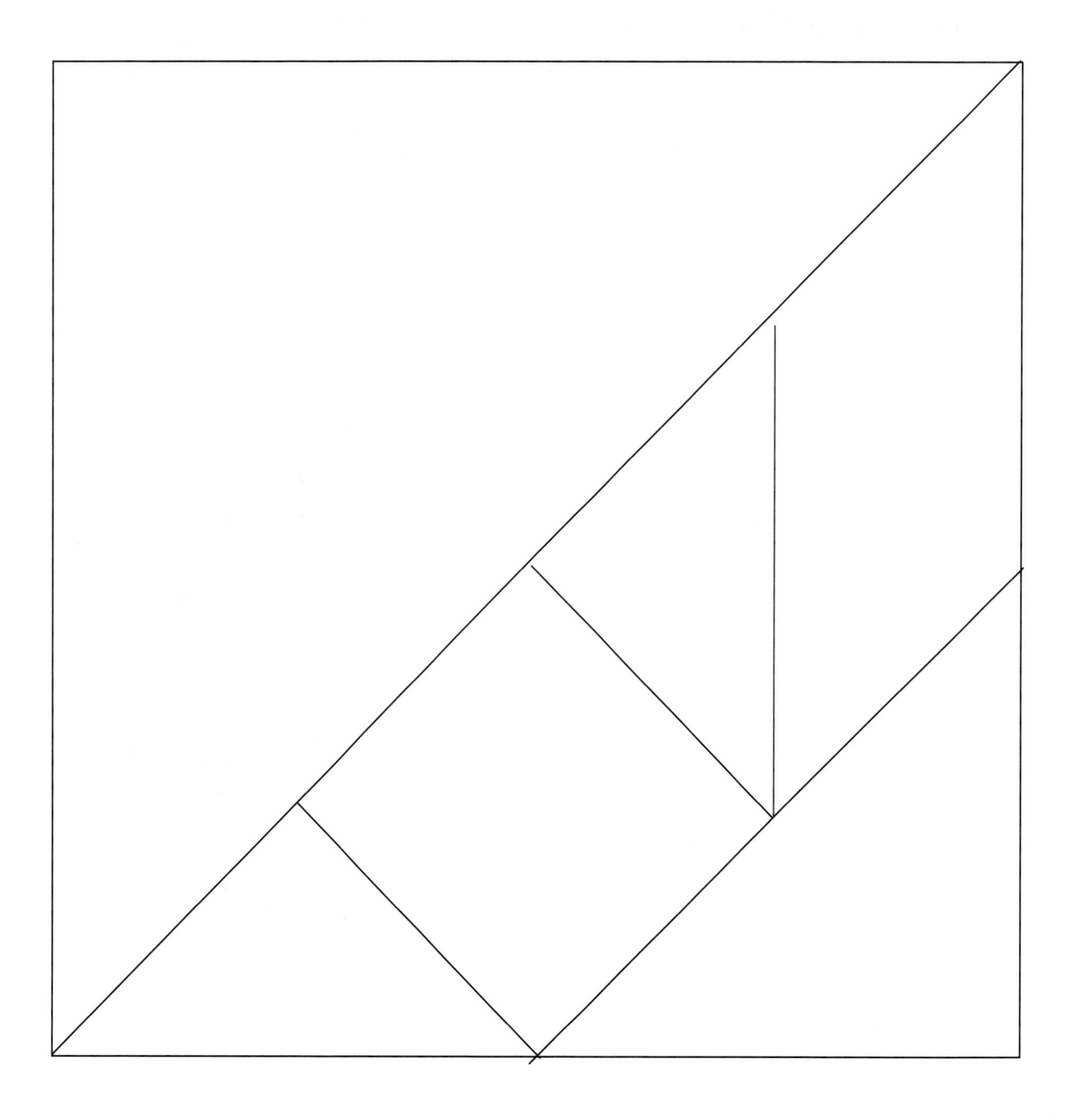

Help for grown-ups:
You may like to cut off the heading and stick it onto another sheet together with your child's picture. The picture must use all the pieces. Colouring may emphasise the picture, too.

Date back to school: _____

Tangram

Introductions

There are several good books that have tangram activities suitable for all ages of children, and a good source of ideas for you. Using an OHP you can show how to disassemble the square and make it into a variety of different shapes or pictures to illustrate the idea. You might wish to suggest that the pictures are on a certain theme, or, together with the title, tell a story. If you have access to the internet in your assembly venue, you could show some of the interactive 'nrich' challenges to provide further ideas.

Extensions/alternatives

You could:
- use a different tangram – for example at spring time you might choose to use the Egg tangram (see below)
- challenge the children to create certain mathematical shapes using all the pieces at any one time eg a large isosceles triangle, or a hexagon
- introduce the children to the stories and challenges from the tangram activities on the 'nrich' web site
- let the children make up their own tangram and offer challenges to their classmates
- with older children label each piece as a fraction of the whole square and ask the children to make a picture using pieces summing to 3/8, 3/4 etc.

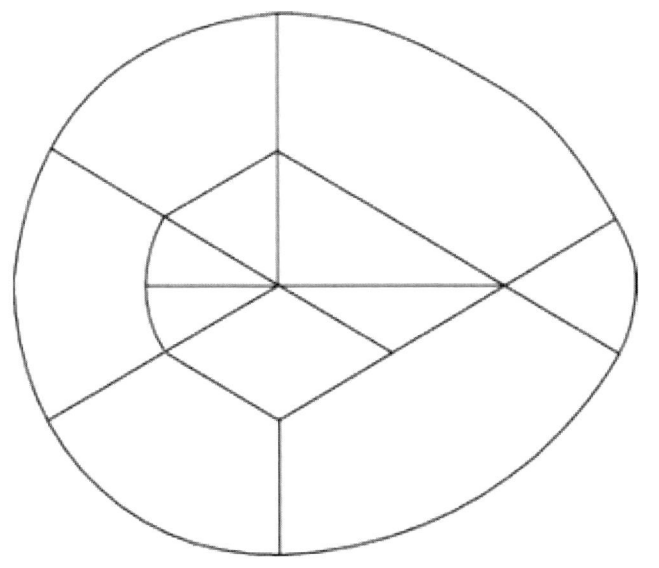

Resources: 🗄 Tangram
🖱 nrich

Cundy and Rollett Egg Tangram

Make a box

What shaped box can you make from one A4 piece of card? You can use lots of sticky tape or glue but no other bits of card!

Name: _____ Class: _____

If you want to make this box copy the net below onto your card. If you want to make a box without a lid, you can leave out the bottom rectangle.

This box uses two circles and one rectangle

This box uses two triangles and three rectangles

Help for grown-ups:
Practice with old card first – the box doesn't have to have lid. You could add some flaps for ease of sticking.

Date back to school: _____

Make a box

Introductions

You could introduce the idea of a net by taking apart several cereal and other boxes. Older children will already have seen nets several times, so you could set a different challenge such as using the card to make the biggest box possible – ie the one with the biggest volume. Emphasise that the whole box must be made from one piece of card only.

Extensions/alternatives

You could:

- set up the interactive display with polydron to make polyhedra, and boxes which can be taken apart
- challenge the children to create boxes which fulfil certain conditions
    - to hold a tennis ball,
    - a cream egg,
    - having a curved face,
    - holding at least a named volume.
- use the boxes to <u>estimate</u> volume
- ask for suggestions for <u>measuring</u> the volume of the various boxes and arrange them in order
- set up an investigation comparing the areas of all the surfaces of a box with the volume.

Resources: 💾 Make a box

Rangoli patterns .... Join the dots to make a doorstep pattern.

Name _____   Class: _____

Name of my pattern: _____

Help for grown-ups:
Rangoli patterns are typically made of coloured powders and painted on the ground on doorsteps by Indian women between Dec 15th and Jan 15th of each year. They are usually symmetrical.

Date back to school: _____

Rangoli

Introductions

Rangoli patterns are made by joining dots arranged in a grid. Usually the patterns have either reflective symmetry or rotational symmetry, and some have both. You could introduce Rangoli patterns by beginning with a single line of symmetry - photocopy the grid opposite and draw a mirror line down the centre, joining the dots. Join dots on one side of the mirror to make a simple pattern and then invite a child to come and draw the reflection. You could then show some other more complicated examples.

Extensions/alternatives

You could:

- challenge the children to bring in symmetrical pictures
- start a display with some Rangoli patterns that have been begun, leaving them for children to complete
- try using coloured sand to make a Rangoli pattern on a board
- suggest that older children use more sophisticated drawing equipment eg rulers and compasses to ensure accuracy
- invite a parent or friend who knows how to do them properly to come and demonstrate.

Resources: Rangoli

illustrations from www.kamat.com

Snail's trails
............Snail needs to go from A to B. How many different paths can he take? What is the shortest? What is the longest path? (He can't use any point more than once, but he doesn't have to use them all. He can't go diagonally – only up or down, or across.)

Name: _____ Class: _____

A

B

Snail's shortest is _____ units   and longest is _____ units

Help for grown-ups:

There are four grids here to have go but you might want to draw a lot more to try different ideas.

Date back to school: _____

50

Snail's trails

Introductions

I like to introduce this using a 3 x 3 array and tell a story about a creature trying to move along the paths from one corner to another. Younger children will enjoy just finding lots of different paths whilst older ones can be encouraged to do this systematically – which may mean inventing some sort of recording code. Don't give any ideas though - let them invent their own. This activity could easily lead on to topology – the study of networks and pathways - the 'nrich' site has a whole section of such linked activities.

Extensions/alternatives

You could:
- ask how many ways there are of getting the longest line and make a display of them
- ask how many ways there are of getting the shortest line and make a display of them
- change the rules so that diagonal lines are allowed
- change the size of the grid to 5 by 5
- change the numbers of times you are allowed to visit each dot
- change the rules so that you have to go over each line joining the dots once and once only. Is it possible?
- ask the children for some 'what ifs' and let them design their own investigations.

Resources: Snails trails

nrich

© nrich website

Matchstick maths

What can you make with 24 matchsticks?

Name: _____ Class: _____

Name of my matchstick challenge: _____

Help for grown-ups:
Of course make sure the match sticks are used ones! 24 is a large number for a young child so you may wish to suggest grouping the matches in some way to make more sense. Try to encourage your child to do something mathematical – it would be relatively easy to make some sort of picture, but a pattern or a puzzle requires more mathematical thinking.

Date back to school: _____

Matchstick maths

Introductions

You could introduce this by putting up a few simple matchstick puzzles on the OHP such as those below. Some children might choose to use all their matchsticks to make a selection of puzzles such as these – they are a good way to encourage the accurate use of mathematical language.

Extensions/alternatives

You could:
- challenge the children to make the widest enclosed shape – the tallest shape – or even a 3-d shape by glueing them together
- use the matches to make numbers and hence sums
- set some challenges – what is the widest 2-d shape that can be made?
- Let the children have a go at making up some puzzles – see 'Maths on fire' for examples.

take way four matches and leave five squares

Resources: Matchstick maths
Maths on fire

Just a minute ....

What can you do in a minute? Write or draw what you found out.

Name: _____   Class: _____

I can:

Help for grown-ups:
The passing of time is a sophisticated concept even to grown-ups. A minute can seem a very long time when you're standing on one leg but no time at all when you're enjoying yourself. Explore some of the more usual and unusual tasks that can be done in a minute.

Date back to school: _____

Just a minute

Introductions

The programme of the same name is introduced by the 'Minute Waltz' by Chopin and if you can get hold of a copy it makes a suitable introduction. Or you could set a stopwatch going, ask everyone to close their eyes and estimate a minute. They put their hands up and open their eyes when they think a minute has gone by. You could ask for a volunteer to come and see if they could stand on one leg for a minute – or see how many times they can bounce a ball... or whatever.

Extensions/alternatives

You could:
- set up a display of different types of clocks with challenges of the 'how long would it take....'questions
- have a sponsored silence
- make a display of time words and everyday sayings to do with time
- play the 'just a minute' game (children have to speak on a given subject for one minute without repetition, deviation or hesitation). You might want to start with half a minute and be quite generous about applying the rules to begin with
- explore sundials and how they work.

Resources: 💾 Just a minute
                       🖱 Sundials

Resources linked to activities

Show a hundred
Million dots poster   www.universalworkshop.com/pages/MIL.htm
10^2 book and poster ACT 029 ATM

Matchboxes
Powers of ten website
www.microcosm.web.cern.ch/microcosm/P10/english/welcome.html
Powers of ten flipbook *Eames and Eames* pub Freeman ISBN 0716734419
Powers of ten *Philip Morrison* pub Freeman ISBN 0716760037

The answer is 6
Numbers, facts, figures and fiction *Richard Phillips* pub Badsey ISBN 095465620-2

Magic Box
Annos mysterious multiplying jar *Anno and Anno* pub Philomel ISBN 0698117530
Counting machine, function machine
www.standards.dfes.gov.uk/numeracy/publications/ict_resources/

Crossword
Make your own crosswords   www.edhelper.com/crossword.htm
Cross number interactive site http://kreuzzahl.de/
Hangman www.interativestuff.org/sums4fun/
Fourbidden card game ACT 012 ATM

What's the question?
Numbers, facts, figures and fiction *Richard Phillips* pub Badsey ISBN 095465620-2

Which Wally
nrich website search under combinatorics www.nrich.maths.org.uk

Nature trail
Fibonacci numbers in nature library.thinkquest.org/27890/applications5.html or
www.mcs.surrey.ac.uk/Personal/R.Knott/Fibonacci/fibnat.html

Circle patterns
nrich website www.nrich.maths.org.uk Path to the Stars (Feb 2002)
smile Inscribe see smilemathematics.co.uk

Show a half
Take part www.standards.dfes.gov.uk/primary/teaching resources/

Christmas maths
The Twelve days of Christmas *John Julius Norwich* pub Transworld ISBN 038541028X

Magic squares
maths forum website mathforum.org/alejandre/magic.square/adler/
magic squares website www.magic-squares.de/magic.html

Stars
Kaleidometrics *Sheillah Shaw* pub Tarquin ISBN 0-906212-21-9 star and other beautiful patterns from circles
Symmetry Patterns *Alan Wiltshire* pub Tarquin ISBN 0-906212-73-1 photocopiable grids to make stars and other symmetrical patterns
Window Patterns *William Gibbs* pub Tarquin ISBN 1-899618-31-7 tissue paper star
Altair creative colouring books pub Longman ISBN -0-582-35040-4 well known grids for spotting patterns including stars
Robert Webb website home.aanet.com.au/robertw/Stellations.html fantastic pictures

What a space!
nrich website search under area www.nrich.maths.org.uk

Pop ups
Up-pops Mark Hiner pub Tarquin ISBN 0-906212-79-0 uses elastic bands to produce
Fractal cuts Diego Uribe pub Tarquin ISBN 0-906212-88-X
www.makersgallery.com/joanirvine/index.html
www.enchantedlearning.com/crafts/cards/flowerpopup/
robertsabuda.com/popmakesimple.asp

Tangram
nrich website search under tangrams www.nrich.maths.org.uk
directory of tangram sites tangrams.ca/inner/diver.htm
Mathworld Weisstein Egg Mathworld

Rangoli patterns
smile website search for Rangoli smilemathematics.co.uk
www.kamat.com/kalranga/rangoli/rangani.htm snaithprimary.eril.net/rangoli.htm

Snail's trails
nrich website search under networks www.nrich.maths.org.uk

Matchstick maths
Maths on Fire: Matchstick Maths *John Dabell* pub Millgate House

Take a minute
www.sundials.co.uk/projects.htm

the NELSON
FIRST CERTIFICATE
workbook

Addison Wesley Longman Ltd.
Edinburgh Gate Harlow
Essex CM20 2JE
and Associated Companies throughout world.

© Susan Morris and Alan Stanton 1996
All rights reserved; no part of this publication
may be reproduced, stored in a retrieval system,
or transmitted in any form or by any means, electronic,
mechanical, photocopying, recording or otherwise,
without the prior written permission of the Publishers.

First published 1996
Second impression 1996

Set in Helvetica 10pt
Printed in Spain
by Gráficas Estella

ISBN 0 17 556920 7

Acknowledgements

We are grateful to the following for permission to reproduce copyright material:

The Associated Press for the articles '14-year-old seeks to scale Everest' by Tim Whitmire page 72, 'Helicopters search sugar cane fields in Florida for five escaped convicts' page 60;
BBC Worldwide for the article 'Come rain or shine' by Kirsty Cockburn page 50;
Rebecca Cripps / *Marie Claire* / Robert Harding Syndication for the article 'Childhood sweethearts' page 39;
Fiona Duff / *BBC Vegetarian Good Food* / Robert Harding Syndication for the article 'Open the box' page 22;
Focus for extracts from the articles 'Go wild in the country' by Ben Webb page 26, 'The law of the gun' page 55, 'Taking on the Ogre' page 78;
The Guardian for the articles 'Self-images: Veronica Webb' by Catherine Wilson page 6, 'Hammer the message home' by Robert Leedham page 15, 'A date with a burglar' by Leslie Jarman page 58;
Celia Haddon for the article 'Thanks for the memory' from *The Daily Telegraph* page 34;
The Independent for the articles 'Maybe it's because they're not Londoners' by Sandra Barwick page 19, 'Painter who lost his sight "sees" as sculptor' by Dalya Alberge page 66, 'The man who lived to tell tales' by Martin Whittaker; page 82;
Los Angeles Times for the article 'Jules Verne's dark vision of modern life' by Scott Kraft page 74;
© Angela Neustatter / The Telegraph plc, London 1994 for the article 'Home life' page 30;
Premiere for the article 'Past lives – Gus van Sant' by Phillipa Bloom © British Premiere Magazine page 70;
Martin Robinson for the article 'Running down Australia's cliffs thrill of lifetime' page 20;
Time Out for the article 'The Time Out guide to fitness' by Andrew Shields page 43;
TNT Magazine for the article 'Riding the rocky road to ruin' page 62;
Usborne Publishing Ltd for the extracts from *The Usborne Book of Inventors* © 1994 Usborne Publishing Ltd page 28 and page 45.

the NELSON
FIRST CERTIFICATE
workbook

Susan Morris, Alan Stanton

LONGMAN

with answers

Contents

Unit 1:	*People and Clothes*	6
Unit 2:	*A Place of Your Own*	10
Unit 3:	*Making a New Start*	14
Unit 4:	*Getting About*	18
Unit 5:	*Cakes and Ale*	22
Unit 6:	*How Things Work*	26
Unit 7:	*The Family*	30
Unit 8:	*Good Companions*	34
Unit 9:	*Emotions and Feelings*	38
Unit 10:	*Making the Most of Yourself*	42
Unit 11:	*Things that Go Wrong*	46
Unit 12:	*Weather and Climate*	50
Unit 13:	*Heroes and Heroines?*	54
Unit 14:	*Victims and Villains*	58
Unit 15:	*Lies, Tricks and Deceit*	62
Unit 16:	*A Thing of Beauty is a Joy Forever*	66
Unit 17:	*A Sense of Achievement*	70
Unit 18:	*Time after Time*	74
Unit 19:	*Exploration, Adventure, Invention*	78
Unit 20:	*Contrasts*	82

unit 1 PEOPLE AND CLOTHES

1 You are going to read an interview with a model. Choose the most suitable heading from the list A–I for each part (1–7) of the article. There is one extra heading which you do not need to use. There is an example at the beginning (0).

A Do you diet?
B Has your appearance affected your career?
C Would you have plastic surgery?
D Do you exercise?
E What image do you have of yourself?
F What kind of clothes do you like?
G Are you aware of fashion?
H What kind of image are you trying to achieve?
I What do you wear to work?

SELF-IMAGES Veronica Webb

Veronica Webb, 28, is Revlon's first black model. She has modelled for ten years, writes a monthly column for *Interview* magazine and presents Fox TVs *Front Page*, a US youth programme.

0	E

A model's image is always changing, so I have to define myself in terms of personality. I think of myself as a capable spokesperson for the company but more than anything I am American.

1	

My appearance is my career.

2	

I like to mix extreme luxury with extreme utility: Levi's with Monolo Blahnik shoes, a good rucksack with a Hermes sweater. I have a designer top five: Azzedine Alaia, Versace, Hermes, Ozbeck and Nike.

3	

When I'm presenting on TV, I like people to concentrate on what I am saying, so I wear a dark blazer with a T-shirt or a white shirt, Levi's and always high heels.

4	

I'm excruciatingly aware of it. I spend more time with clothes than with the people I love.

5	

When my schedule allows, I roller-blade and swim.

6	

Every once in a while, when I've been home for the holidays and my Ma has fed me up with pancakes.

7	

The idea of someone putting a knife into my healthy flesh is horrific.

unit **1** PEOPLE AND CLOTHES

2 Complete the sentences with the appropriate verb – *put on, take off, wear* or *carry* – in the correct form.

EXAMPLE: It was so cold when I went into the building that I didn't *take off* my coat.

1 When last seen, the old lady was walking down the street, ... a blue dress and .... a basket of shopping.

2 Have you decided what to .... to the party?

3 The weather was hot, so when Lucy got dressed, she .... a pair of shorts and a T-shirt.

4 I always .... an umbrella in case it rains.

5 The bag of groceries was so heavy that I found it difficult to ....

6 What do you .... when you go to bed?

7 It was snowing outside, so I .... an extra sweater.

8 Have you ever .... glasses?

9 The doctor wanted to examine the patient and asked him to .... his jacket.

10 Mary likes to .... her long hair loose.

3 Complete the sentences with the appropriate verb – *suit, match* or *fit* – in the correct form.

EXAMPLE: Jane has such big feet that it's difficult for her to find shoes that *fit* .

1 I liked the dress very much but when I tried it on, it just didn't .... me.

2 The bow in Mary's hair .... her pretty party dress.

3 Narrow-legged trousers .... Mark best.

4 Shirley was wearing a green dress with a .... jacket.

5 Blue is a colour that really .... Anthea.

6 Find a hairstyle that .... you and stick with it.

7 Tom carried a handkerchief that .... his tie.

8 I'll have to lose weight, otherwise my summer clothes will just not ....

9 These latest fashions just don't .... me.

10 This shade of green is a difficult colour to ....

4 Fill the gaps with the adjectives which occur at the end of the sentences, making sure that the order is correct.

EXAMPLE: These *fluffy wool* sweaters are very fashionable this season. FLUFFY WOOL

1 Tina looked at the cloudy sky and put on a .... jacket. LONG SHOWERPROOF

2 The actress had to wear .... clothes for her part in the new play. OLD SHABBY

3 Everyone comments on Anne's .... hair. SHINY WAIST-LENGTH

4 All the children had been told to wear .... boots. RUBBER WATERPROOF

5 Ian spent all the money he had left on two .... shirts. DESIGNER EXPENSIVE

6 In hot weather, there's nothing better than .... clothing. COOL COTTON

7 The film-star appeared at the film premiere in a .... dress. BLACK TIGHT

8 Alice thought that her grand-daughter looked very sweet in her .... dress. NEW PRETTY

9 Knowing how dirty he would get digging the garden, Fred put on his oldest gardening clothes, a .... shirt and a pair of .... trousers. CHECK GREEN/BAGGY BROWN

10 The secretary's .... jacket looked as if it had never been ironed. CREASED LINEN

5 Read the text below and think of the word which best fits each space. There is an example at the beginning (0).

The well-dressed cowboy

The basic clothes of an American cowboy in the second half of the nineteenth century consisted (0) ...of... a cotton shirt and woollen trousers. Levi jeans, now part of the cowboy image, did not (1) .... popular until the early twentieth century. Most of the things a cowboy wore (2) .... determined by the nature of the job he was (3) .... Waistcoats (4) .... deep pockets were popular because it is difficult to put your hands in your trouser pockets (5) .... on horseback. Cowboys often had to ride through thorn bushes, (6) .... would tear clothes and skin, so they wore long leather leggings or 'chaps' ((7) .... the Mexican word *chaparreras*). A cowboy's hat was a good guide to (8) .... he was working. In the south-west, hats were high and wide to provide good protection (9) .... the sun. Further north, hats were smaller and therefore less (10) .... to be blown off by strong cold winds. Hats (11) .... also be used to carry water and to start a fire. Cowboys wore bandannas round their necks (12) .... a protection against sunburn and also to cover (13) .... mouths when the cattle kicked up a lot of dust. Contrary to popular belief, they rarely wore guns (14) .... guns were too heavy and uncomfortable to wear when riding a horse (15) .... day.

6 Read the text below and look carefully at each line. Some of the lines are correct and some have a word which should not be there. Write the wrong word in the space provided and tick the correct lines. There are two examples at the beginning (0) and (00).

FATHER AND SON

Angus Cameron is thirteen years old and his father Stephen — 0 ✓

is twenty-five years older. Is there a lot difference in the — 00 lot

clothes they wear? Most of the week Angus must to wear — 1 must

grey trousers and a red blazer. It's compulsory for to wear — 2 for

this uniform at his school. In his free time, he likes to — 3 ✓

wear the jeans and a sweatshirt. Stephen does too, but he — 4 the

can only do so on Saturday and Sunday. The bank at where — 5 at

he works expects him to dress himself in a suit with a shirt — 6 himself

and tie. Both father and son like to keep their fit so on — 7 their

Saturday they go jogging all together in the park in their — 8 all

tracksuits. They also would like to play football with friends — 9 ✓

and for this they wear shorts, shirts in the colours of their — 10 ✓

favourite team and boots. With the other members of the family — 11 ✓

they plan to go out skiing in January and they have — 12 ✓

been buying clothes which they think are being both warm — 13 being

and fashionable. They want to be able to wear such clothes — 14 ✓

in the street as well as on the ski slopes too. — 15 too

unit 2 A PLACE OF YOUR OWN

1 You are going to read a magazine article about people and rooms they think are special. For questions 1–16, choose from the people (A–D). Some of the people may be used more than once. When more than one answer is required, these may be given in any order.

Which of the people

has reminders of the family in the room?	1	....
has provided a substantial area of working space?	2	....
likes having refreshments in the room?	3	....
sometimes invites people to the room?	4	....
made a conscious decision not to have much decoration?	5	....
relaxes by listening to music?	6	....
has a room at the top of the house?	7	8 ....
has objects from childhood in the room?	9	10 ....
had to make major improvements in order to use the room?	11	....
uses the room for work and relaxation?	12	13 ....
refuses people permission to enter?	14	....
has a room at the bottom of the house?	15	....
loved the room from the start?	16	....

A HARRY EBWORTH
B JUNE TITMARSH
C TERRY HENCHARD
D VICTORIA EMERSON

A room of one's own

Why is it that men and women are insisting more and more on a room of their own – a private space they can design and decorate according to their personal taste, a place where they can relax, away from family pressures?

Academic Harry Ebworth bought his house in a small village in Oxfordshire ten years ago:
'When we came to view the house, the thing that was really amazing was that when you came in through the front door you went up the stairs and then went up again and you seemed to go on and on climbing. And at the top of the house there was this marvellous room, so light and airy. The room might look a bit untidy at first glance, but I know exactly where everything is and it's actually very well-organised. I've got a purpose-built work surface along one wall, with shelving underneath. That's where I've got my computer, the printer and the modem for communicating by e-mail. Opposite that, on the other side of the room, I've got my working table. It's actually a draughtsman's table so it's tilted, and I do all my creative writing there. I mustn't forget to mention my armchair, a modern chair made of black leather and chrome. It's lovely to relax and think in.'

School governor June Titmarsh lives in Herefordshire:
'Our house is always busy – the children (June has four) are always in and out with their friends and Tom (her husband) runs his business from home. I needed a place where I could be by myself. We had this cellar under the house, and it was dark and uninviting, and I didn't see what practical use we could make of it as a family. So I thought, right, this is going to be my space. I had the floor relaid with terracotta tiles, which are a lovely rich colour, and the walls are painted white. The biggest luxury was the sofa – I wanted something that was really comfortable and relaxing, and with this one, I can stretch out and close my eyes or curl up and read a book. I've kept the decoration to a minimum, as we have lots of paintings and knick-knacks in the rest of the house, but I've got some of my favourite photographs of the children on the walls. This is my bolt-hole. No one is EVER allowed in.'

Musician Terry Henchard lives in south London:
'Our house is unusual because it was built to our own design and makes a lot of use of glass. The bedrooms are on the ground floor and the living-space is on the first floor. I found I couldn't really relax upstairs – the sitting room is just too big and impersonal. So I looked around the house and found this area under the stairs which has good lighting because of the windows but still feels cosy and intimate. I moved in my stereo and the TV and when I want to be alone, I retreat to my 'den', put my feet up and listen to music. I can also keep things here which look out of place in the rest of the house, silly things like my first piggy bank, the half-size violin on which I learnt to play and the photo of me in the school cricket team. It's important to me to have this personal space, somewhere where no one comes unless specifically invited.'

Victoria Emerson is a writer and lives in Hampstead:
'My room is both my relaxing space and my working space, which in some ways is not ideal. I decided to have the TV and video up here (Victoria's study is at the top of the house in a renovated attic) because I didn't want them downstairs where we use the rooms for entertaining. There isn't much room for hanging pictures but I've got some photos of people I admire. I don't have a coffee-maker up here, but I've got a lovely brass table where I can put the coffee that I make downstairs. I've got lots of the teddy bears and cuddly toys that I had when I was young. They cut down the sense of isolation you get when you spend lots of time working on your own.

unit **2** A PLACE OF YOUR OWN

2 Read the text below and decide which answer (A, B, C or D) best fits each space. Put a circle round the letter that you choose. The exercise begins with an example (0).

Australian Couple's Antarctic Home

Dan and Margie McIntyre, who enjoy the challenge of (**0**) .... adventure, are about to (**1**) .... home in the Antarctic. Not only is it in the Antarctic but in one of the most (**2**) .... places in that (**3**) .... , Commonwealth Bay. It is here that the famous polar explorer, Douglas Mawson, (**4**) .... two years of hardship earlier this century. Mawson almost died because of the (**5**) .... weather conditions. His wooden hut still stands and the McIntyres intend to (**6**) .... photographs of it. Their own hut, which they are taking with them, is made of fibre-glass and measures 2.5 metres (**7**) .... 3.5 metres. It will be fixed to the (**8**) .... in order to (**9**) .... it from being blown away by the (**10**) .... winds, which blow at 300 kph and make it impossible to go out for weeks at a time.

The McIntyres will (**11**) .... in touch with the (**12**) .... world via a computer network and hope to (**13**) .... their experiences to schoolchildren in many countries. They will stay for a year but will take enough food for two in case ships cannot (**14**) .... to them because of sea ice. They intend to take all their rubbish back to Australia, including the hut, so that no (**15**) .... of them remains in Antarctica.

0	A	great	B	big	C	dramatic	D	high
1	A	set off	B	set up	C	set down	D	set in
2	A	inhospitable	B	unwelcome	C	inconvenient	D	unfriendly
3	A	country	B	district	C	part	D	region
4	A	endured	B	had	C	lasted	D	did
5	A	wild	B	severe	C	critical	D	hard
6	A	make	B	record	C	have	D	take
7	A	by	B	times	C	from	D	of
8	A	site	B	soil	C	ground	D	land
9	A	prevent	B	hold	C	resist	D	strengthen
10	A	fast	B	strong	C	savage	D	furious
11	A	keep	B	be	C	have	D	make
12	A	external	B	outer	C	other	D	outside
13	A	describe	B	give	C	share	D	teach
14	A	journey	B	get	C	voyage	D	move
15	A	trace	B	mark	C	pollution	D	feature

3 Complete the second sentence so that it has a similar meaning to the first sentence. Use the word given and other words to complete each sentence. You must use between two and five words. Do not change the word given.

EXAMPLE: John didn't know the answer to the question.
no
John ....*had no idea*.... what the answer to the question was.

1 You haven't seen this play before, have you?
first
This .... you have seen this play, isn't it?

2 You can choose any one you like.
matter
It doesn't .... choose.

3 'I don't advise you to go there alone,' said Peter.
myself
Peter said that .... wasn't a good idea.

4 This dog hasn't been fed for three days.
was
It's three days .... fed.

5 Students must clean their own rooms.
responsible
Students .... their own rooms.

6 This is the best microscope you can buy.
better
You .... microscope than this one.

7 I didn't know what your feelings were on this matter.
how
I had no idea .... about this matter.

8 I can't tell you the number because I can only just see the bus.
hardly
I .... the bus, let alone the number.

9 When I suggested the idea, Jack did not object at all.
no
Jack .... to the idea I suggested.

10 We'd like to discuss these proposals with you for a few minutes.
word
We'd like .... with you about the new proposals.

4 Write questions based on the following sentences, using the words given.

EXAMPLE: David won first prize?
ANSWER: *Who won first prize?*
ANSWER: *What did David win?*

1 Margaret won a prize for her first novel.
a Who ....
b What ....

2 Mr Thomas started the meeting at 10 a.m.
a Who ....
b When ....

3 The rocket crashed into the sea.
a What ....
b Where ....

4 Thousands of people bought lottery tickets.
a How many ....
b What ....

5 Martin spent three years in prison.
a Who ....
b How long ....

6 Mrs Jones cooked us plenty of food.
a Who ....
b How much ....

7 Simon met many interesting people at the conference.
a Who ....
b Where ....

8 The manager cancelled the race because of fog.
a Who ....
b Why ....

unit **2** A PLACE OF YOUR OWN

13

unit 3 MAKING A NEW START

1 You are going to read a newspaper article about the advice on careers that people were given at school. For questions 1–15, choose from the list of people (A–H). Some of the names may be used more than once. When more than one answer is required, these may be given in any order.

Which person

was discouraged from choosing a desired career? 1 .... 2 ....

thinks students should assess their own abilities? 3 ....

thinks the advice might have been better in another part of the country? 4 ....

felt other students in the school received better advice? 5 ....

was not attracted by the careers suggested? 6 .... 7 ....

says no careers advice was available? 8 ....

respects the advice given by teachers? 9 ....

considers the idea of careers advice in school as inappropriate? 10 ....

thinks the best advice about professions comes from those actually doing the job? 11 ....

went to a school that developed their particular talents? 12 ....

was upset by the advice given? 13 ....

thinks good careers advice depends on knowing the person looking for advice? 14 .... 15 ....

A JOHN BECKETT
B DANIELLE LUX
C MARK MOORE
D SHAMI AHMED
E CAROL VORDERMAN
F ALAN SMITH
G LESLIE JOSEPH
H JIMMY NAIL

Hammer the message home

Today's careers adviser, like John Beckett, is a highly-trained specialist but actor and singer Jimmy Nail and many of those interviewed below have achieved success in spite of the advice they received at school.

John Beckett
Careers adviser

My careers advice at school was a ten-minute interview about opportunities in banking and insurance – two career areas I had no interest in at all. After university I remembered this experience and thought that there must be a better way of doing this. So I trained to become a careers adviser.

Over the past few years I have worked with many other careers advisers who have an up-to-date knowledge of jobs, training and further and higher-education opportunities.

Giving good careers advice is all about getting to know your clients well, finding out their needs, giving them accurate information and offering support and encouragement while they try to achieve their aims.

Reading careers literature is one thing but getting up-to-date advice from an expert should put any student on the right track.

Danielle Lux
Presenter of BBC2 television's Rough Guide To Careers, producer of Dance Energy and The Word

At school they were only interested in people who were going to university. I always knew I wanted to do something like acting or being in front of a camera. They blocked the idea of me going to drama school. I suppose they had no resources to tell me how to go about it.

Mark Moore
Disc jockey and pop star

I don't see how a complete stranger can help you choose your career. Surely you need someone who knows you quite well. I didn't know what I wanted to do. I was interested in films and music, and I thought things would just fall into place. When I left school, I took a year off, and started going to clubs regularly.

Shami Ahmed
Owner of The Legendary Joe Bloggs Jeans Company; turnover £30 million

Even at the age of 14, I knew I could do things for myself, could make them happen in the real world. That's the real test – after you leave the classroom. Other people can't tell you your strengths and weaknesses, you have to work them out for yourself.

Carol Vorderman
Statistician, member of Mensa, the organisation for people who are exceptionally intelligent, director of educational video company

I wanted to do engineering but I was stuck in this little rural school in Wales. If I'd been living in Manchester, maybe they would have known what to tell me. But even at Cambridge University, where I studied engineering, the attitude was 'sink or swim' – you had to use your initiative to find your way. It's always better to hear things from the horse's mouth. The real person who does that job can tell you about the real pains and joys of the job.

Alan Smith
Football player, has 3 A levels and speaks three languages

I went to a grammar school that was very sports-oriented, but the teachers always advised us to concentrate on good exam results first. It was good advice, and I started a degree, but I didn't finish my course because Leicester Football Club offered me a contract in the middle of it.

Leslie Joseph
Actress

There was no careers advice whatsoever in my school. Maybe some students did have a teacher talk to them, but there were no lessons or anything formal. I certainly didn't get any useful information about becoming an actress, although it was my headmistress who actually spotted what she called 'my potential'. She told me I should go on the stage.

Jimmy Nail
Actor and singer

I hated my careers teacher. He told me I would never get any O levels, never mind a job. When I said I wanted to be a teacher, he said: 'For kids like you there are three alternatives – the building site, the pit or the boatyard. You'd better get used to that.' I went off the rails, school-wise. I was expelled for burning it down, even though it was an accident – I was playing with a magnifying glass in assembly and the curtains caught fire.

SETTLING IN

Things are going very well here. My new job is everything I   0 ✓

expected it to be and I have so quickly settled in. The flat   00 so

where I am staying is very comfortable but I have had to spend   1 ....

a lot of time sorting out to domestic arrangements. For example   2 ....

there was no any telephone at first but I have now arranged for   3 ....

one to be installed. In four days' time I should soon be able to   4 ....

phone you and tell you my new number. I also had to get the   5 ....

gas and electricity connected with. Of course, that had to be done   6 ....

on the very first day. There wasn't much of furniture in the flat, only   7 ....

basic things like a bed and a table so I've bought a few things of   8 ....

my own. It's second-hand but it's in the good condition and it was   9 ....

remarkably cheap. I am still need a few pictures to put on the walls   10 ....

because at the moment they are quite bare which makes that the   11 ....

flat look a bit rather bleak. I'm going to buy some carpets and   12 ....

cushions too in order to make the place live more comfortable. In   13 ....

a few weeks' time it should look and feel like real home. When it   14 ....

does, I'll invite you here for the weekend if you might like.   15 ....

unit **3** MAKING A NEW START

3 Complete the second sentence so that it has a similar meaning to the first sentence. Use the word given and other words to complete each sentence. You must use between two and five words. Do not change the word given.

1 Mrs Jones had twins last December.
 birth
 Mrs Jones ....
 twins last December.

2 The children's computer game looks so interesting I'd like to try it.
 go
 The children's computer game looks so interesting I'd like ....
 myself.

3 Do we have to bring our own food?
 necessary
 Is it .... bring our own food?

4 I think it's best if I take a taxi to my house.
 home
 I think it's best if I ....
 .... taxi.

5 Leave now or I'll call the police.
 you
 If .... now, I'll call the police.

6 I'm sorry I didn't warn you in time.
 apologise
 I .... you in time.

7 I recommend that you pay the price he is asking.
 had
 In my opinion, you ....
 .... the price he is asking.

8 It's Mark's job to arrange the party.
 arrangements
 Mark will .... the party.

9 Jenny has not decided on her future career.
 decision
 Jenny has ....
 about her future career.

10 The spectators were astonished at how determined the athletes were.
 by
 The spectators were astonished at ....
 .... the athletes.

4 Complete the sentences with a phrasal verb based on *go*.

EXAMPLE: The temperature *went down* as winter approached.

1 The pupils .... talking even though the teacher had asked them to stop.

2 Michael and Claire .... together for three months, then they split up.

3 All the young people in the village .... to get jobs in big cities as soon as they have left school.

4 Following a big advertising campaign, sales of the product .... by 25 per cent.

5 I was quietly reading in bed when suddenly the light ....

6 If you eat too much of one thing you're likely to .... it.

7 At this time of year the sun .... after nine o'clock at night.

8 If you really think this is the job for you, you should .... it.

9 The alarm .... as the burglar tried to climb in through the window.

10 After her success in school drama productions, Mary decided to .... acting as a career.

17

unit 4

GETTING ABOUT

1 You are going to read a newspaper article about people in London. For questions 1–14, choose from the list of people (A–G). Some of the answers may be used more than once. When more than one answer is required, these may be given in any order.

Which of the visitors to London			
appreciated what could be looked at?		1	
commented on cleanliness?		2	
appreciated London's transport facilities?	3	4	
had travelled elsewhere in Britain?	5	6	
were addressed in their own language?		7	
used a sense other than sight to appreciate the city?		8	
enjoyed feeling a sense of the past?	9	10	
had been impressed by the animals in Britain?		11	
had the chance to enjoy good weather?		12	
had plans for further visits to famous sights?		13	
expressed surprise at the lack of eye-contact?		14	

A Elizabeth Barck
B Bob and Simonne Hoggarth
C Jane Carruthers
D Carol Turoff
E The Dupont family
F Petra Schmidt and Wolfgang Muller
G Eileen Larkin

18

Maybe it's because they're not Londoners

PIGEONS, a column, a fountain, a few hundred people with video cameras on their shoulders: in Trafalgar Square there was everything a tourist might expect. Except Londoners. The tourists were in the same capital, of course, but a very different London from the workaday version.

It was as though a clear plastic dome lay over them, cutting off the life of the city outside. You should have been able to pick up the whole square, like a snowstorm toy from one of the cheap souvenir shops on the edge of the square, and shake it, until all the pigeons rose into the air and floated, glittering, round Nelson's head.

Elizabeth Barck, from Sydney, was gazing upwards within this curious world, entranced. 'I just love tradition!' she confessed. 'I could sit here for hours and look at Nelson on his column. We're going to look at Buckingham Palace next.'

Bob and Simonne Hoggarth from Vancouver, Canada, were standing nearby, smiling. 'It's a whole lot cleaner than other capital cities we've visited,' they said. 'And people have been a lot friendlier. We thought it would be really dirty, and people would be impolite. And we love your taxis. We got a very polite taxi driver. He was unbelievably friendly.'

By the Thames, the Tower of London rose, white and grey against grey skies. A woman from New Zealand, Jane Carruthers, waiting in the queue for tickets said she had been all over England, Wales, Ireland and Scotland in 23 days and what had struck her most was the Lake District sheep. 'They were wonderful!' she said. 'Black faces! We have a lot of sheep in New Zealand, but none as pretty as yours.' We walked towards the Middle Tower. In the tourist shop, teddy-bear versions of Yeoman Warders were on sale, and, indeed, the Yeoman Warders, plump and jovial, seemed uniformly teddy-bear-like.

Carol Turoff, from Arizona, was admiring the guardsman outside Waterloo Barracks. His eyes were glazed. She was staying in Leamington Spa, and she was puzzled by the people there. 'They avert their eyes if you're passing by on the sidewalk,' she said. 'In Phoenix, they say hello.' But this had not dented her enthusiasm. 'Your tube is wonderful!' she said. 'And the ticket collectors on your British Rail trains are so helpful! And the history here is just fabulous.'

The crowds flowed out of the Tower. The Dupont family from Lille were sitting in the sun outside a coffee shop. It was called 'Enough 2 feed an Elephant'. The waitresses were smiling. One of them was talking to a German couple, Petra Schmidt and Wolfgang Muller, in German. It was true, through tourist eyes, the capital was friendly. In clean, tidy, renovated Leicester Square, two policemen in shirt sleeves were smiling and chatting in the sunshine to a litter collector. You could buy a plastic version of their helmets round the corner to remind you how helpful they were.

I threaded my way through the happy crowds on Shaftesbury Avenue. Hidden in a shop door, a punk girl was desperately slapping the face of a half-unconscious young man. On cue, a shiny red London bus arrived, with a friendly conductor, to deliver shop girls back to the grey, pollution-hung streets where Londoners live and dream of moving to the country. In Leicester Square, Eileen Larkin from Dublin was sniffing with relish. 'It's diesel and burgers and cigars and warmth,' she said. 'I love the smell of this place.'

For tourists breathe different air.

2 Read the text below and think of the word which best fits each space. Use only one word in each space. The exercise begins with an example (0).

RAP-JUMPING

Rap-jumping involves descending a cliff face, but *not* backwards facing (**0**) __the__ rock. (**1**) _____, you walk to the cliff edge and, holding a rope between your fingers, you just run down the cliff. The magic trick is (**2**) _____ a rope is looped (**3**) _____ a ring in your waist harness in a special figure-of-eight pattern, and that finger pressure on the rope (**4**) _____ stop your descent.

We were at the top of a 50-metre gorge. Our instructor demonstrated (**5**) _____ to do. He walked to the edge, gripped the rope and leaned forward and outward. Then he released the rope and started walking down the cliff. When he wanted to stop he pressed the rope (**6**) _____ just his thumb and finger. Then it was (**7**) _____ turn. It was scary standing at the top of a high cliff. Frightening thoughts flashed (**8**) _____ my mind – the rope could break, the ring could break, I could slip… I hesitated, my legs felt weak, I was trying to find courage from (**9**) _____ .

'It's mind (**10**) _____ matter,' our instructor said. 'You won't come to (**11**) _____ harm.' I (**12**) _____ go of the rope and took a little jump down the cliff. There was (**13**) _____ turning back now. I took some more little jumps and I was on (**14**) _____ way. My confidence grew and I was going quite fast by the time I reached the bottom. It was a thrill – I just wanted to go back up and do it (**15**) _____ .

unit 4 GETTING ABOUT

3 Complete the second sentence so that it has a similar meaning to the first sentence. Use the word given and other words to complete each sentence. You must use between two and five words. Do not change the word given.

1 I am surprised at how many people have come to the meeting.
   expect
   I .... people to come to the meeting.

2 Can you help me to translate this letter?
   give
   I'd like you to .... translating this letter.

3 The minister does not intend to comment on these rumours.
   no
   The minister .... on these rumours.

4 Who is responsible for preparing for the Prime Minister's visit?
   charge
   Who is .... preparing for the Prime Minster's visit?

5 We were astonished when he refused to help us.
   his
   We were astonished .... to help us.

6 I do not regret my decision.
   no
   I have .... my decision.

7 The explorers realised that they would never find the treasure.
   hope
   The explorers gave .... the treasure.

8 'When I started to play football, my father encouraged me a lot,' said Gary.
   plenty
   'My father gave me .... when I started to play football,' said Gary.

9 Does the owner allow you to fish in this lake?
   permission
   Do you .... to fish in this lake?

10 Has Abigail invited you to her party?
   received
   Have .... Abigail's party?

4 Complete the sentences with a phrasal verb based on *keep*.

EXAMPLE: People using the park are requested to ......*keep off*...... the grass.

1 There was a notice at the entrance to the military establishment warning people to ....

2 The other students seem much cleverer than me and I find it hard to ....

3 Margaret wanted to .... the bad news .... her daughter.

4 John .... asking Sally to go out with him but she doesn't want to.

5 Martin found it difficult to .... the payments on the loan.

6 Once John has made a commitment, you can be sure he'll .... it.

7 We ask people who visit the garden to .... the paths.

8 When the manager is in this kind of mood it's best for people to ....

9 The animals are allowed in the garden during the day but are .... at night.

10 Anna was full of good intentions when she started the diet, but finds it difficult to .... it ....

unit 5 CAKES AND ALE

1 You are going to read a magazine article about a way of obtaining fruit and vegetables. Choose the most suitable heading from the list A–H for each part (1–7). There is one extra heading which you do not need to use.

A	What's in the Box?	D	A Growing Business	G	Involving the Customer
B	Mixed Blessings	E	How it Works	H	Helping the Community
C	A Typical Customer	F	Something for Everyone		

Open the box

At first glance, choosing to buy organic fruit and vegetables, that is fruit and vegetables grown without the use of any chemicals, may seem like an option open only to the privileged few. Through the Vegebox scheme, however, producers can deliver wholesome, healthy goods at competitive prices – and they'll even bring them to your home!

1

By Thursday morning each week, the vegetable rack in the Smith household is completely empty. But mother-of-two Julie never has to make a long journey into town to restock. She knows that by the evening it will be brimming with fresh organic vegetables. For Julie is one of the people now shopping the Vegebox way.

2

Vegebox schemes are growing in popularity. They allow you to buy straight from the grower, cutting out a trip to the shops, and let you stock up on fresh, seasonal local produce. The process is simple. Once a week, a van pulls up at the co-ordinator's home and unloads boxes of fresh fruit and vegetables. Customers like Julie then arrive at the co-ordinator's house, eager to see what their Vegebox holds this week. Members of this particular scheme can choose a £3, £5 or £10 box of vegetables. They telephone their order on Sunday, then sit back and wait.

3

You never know exactly what you'll get each week but every box guarantees at least six seasonal vegetables. 'Sometimes I might get a cabbage and think "What am I going to do with this?" But it makes cooking so interesting,' says Julie. It also seems to have improved the family's health and taste buds.

4

Not all Vegebox customers are young families. Members include students, people with special dietary needs and others who have difficulty getting to the shops. With customers no more than a 10-minute walk away and growers delivering in person, there's an added social bonus. 'It's a good way to get to know your neighbours,' says Julie. 'And I like the idea of having close contact with the people who grow your food. I feel you can trust it more.'

5

Arnold Warneken and Alexandra Marsh never imagined the success of their Vegebox scheme. Eighteen months ago they started delivering home-grown vegetables. The first order was for thirteen boxes. By the summer they were working flat out to fill 250 boxes. They originally started growing vegetables for their own use, intending to share the surplus with friends. But things progressed. Arnold gave up his job and Alex devoted herself to the business too. They now grow most of the Vegebox vegetables themselves, concentrating on seasonal produce. They specialise in summer crops such as tomatoes, peppers, and salad leaves.

6

They see their roles as far greater than supplying people with organic food. Their vision for the future is to boost the local economy. 'We have prices that are equal to what you pay in the supermarket, but you're getting organic produce, which is better, healthier and delivered to the doorstep,' says Arnold. 'And if people aren't going to the supermarket for their fruit and veg, they may say it's not worth going for other things and start using local shops again.'

7

But while Vegebox has brought Arnold and Alexandra health and happiness, it hasn't brought great financial rewards. 'The scheme has been wonderful for us and lots of others, but it hasn't made us money,' says Alex. 'We do it because we strongly believe in it.'

2 Read the text below. Use the word given in capitals at the end of each line to form a word that fits in the space in the same line. There is an example at the beginning (0).

WRITING ABOUT FOOD

Apicius, who lived in ancient Rome, is the first (0) __cookery__ book **COOK**

writer (1) .... to historians. Some of the recipes in his book are **KNOW**

unusual. One describes how to stuff (2) .... Medieval books **MOUSE**

contain recipes for food which is (3) .... spiced, as well as **HEAVY**

unfamiliar (4) .... of fruit and meat. The taste of the meat, which **COMBINE**

could have been almost (5) ...., was disguised (we hope!) by the **ROT**

(6) .... of strong flavourings. In the nineteenth century, books such **ADD**

as *Mrs Beeton's Book of Household* (7) .... became popular. It **MANAGE**

is still in print today, but with (8) .... to bring it up to date. Modern **REVISE**

writers make (9) .... on television in order to give demonstrations **APPEAR**

of their recipes and offer (10) .... on cooking techniques. **ADVISE**

unit **5** CAKES AND ALE

3 Read the text below and decide which answer (A, B, C or D) best fits each space. Put a circle round the letter that you choose. The exercise begins with an example (0).

Chocolate

Chocolate is an excellent (**0**) .... of energy. It also (**1**) .... many vitamins and some caffeine. It first became known to Europeans when Spanish conquistadors brought it back from Mexico (**2**) .... in the sixteenth century. The word 'chocolate' (**3**) .... from the Aztec word *xocoatl*. The Aztecs consumed it in the (**4**) .... of a very bitter drink. In Europe, it was drunk with sugar to (**5**) .... it more palatable. Chocolate was popular in Spain and France (**6**) .... before it became popular in Britain. The first chocolate shop in London, (**7**) .... by a Frenchman, (**8**) .... in 1657 but prices were very high and it was not until the nineteenth century, when prices were much lower, that the (**9**) .... for chocolate increased in Britain. Until that time chocolate was always made into a drink and not eaten in (**10**) .... form but by the middle of the nineteenth century chocolate bars for eating, milk chocolate and chocolate-coated biscuits were all (**11**) .... available in shops.

About 50 per cent of the world's (**12**) .... of cocoa beans, from which chocolate is made, comes from Africa and a further 25 per cent from South America. The best quality chocolate has a (**13**) .... proportion of cocoa beans, at least 60 per cent, and tastes quite bitter. Although connoisseurs of (**14**) .... chocolate prefer this sort, many people, unaccustomed to such a (**15**) .... taste, find it too bitter and prefer cheaper, sweeter chocolate with only 20 per cent of cocoa beans in it.

0	A	means	B	product	C	source	D	sort
1	A	holds	B	contains	C	offers	D	delivers
2	A	presently	B	just	C	soon	D	early
3	A	comes	B	develops	C	changes	D	gets
4	A	custom	B	shape	C	style	D	form
5	A	taste	B	make	C	enjoy	D	have
6	A	much	B	greatly	C	long	D	mainly
7	A	owned	B	possessed	C	patronised	D	maintained
8	A	ran	B	established	C	opened	D	set
9	A	demand	B	appeal	C	order	D	call
10	A	blocked	B	hard	C	shaped	D	solid
11	A	largely	B	completely	C	totally	D	widely
12	A	stock	B	quantity	C	supply	D	amount
13	A	great	B	high	C	major	D	big
14	A	nice	B	fine	C	pure	D	best
15	A	deep	B	dark	C	spicy	D	strong

The answer to 0 is C (source).

4 Choose the correct word for the gap in each sentence. The two words are not necessarily in the correct order.

EXAMPLE: **hardly hard**
a Tim worked very ....hard.... to make his company successful.
b There were ....hardly.... any people on the beach.

1 **permit permission**
a The guards asked to see my ....
b If you wish to leave work early, you must ask the manager for ....

2 **although despite**
a .... the bad weather, Chris went for his regular daily run.
b .... he didn't have much experience, Tom applied for the job.

3 **checked controlled**
a The doorman .... everybody's tickets.
b New traffic lights .... the movement of vehicles.

4 **interesting profitable**
a Visitors to the trade fair found the company's new products very ....
b It is a fascinating product but it will not be .... for our company.

5 **marks notes**
a Jack got very high .... in all his exam papers.
b These lecture .... are easy to understand.

6 **wounded injured**
a The driver of the car was .... in the crash but not the passengers.
b There were many .... soldiers on the battlefield.

7 **sensible sensitive**
a This cream is ideal for .... skin.
b Mrs Brown told the children to be .... and not silly.

8 **advice advise**
a Professor Moore gave me some excellent ....
b I need a lawyer to .... me on this matter.

9 **fit suit**
a This hat doesn't .... very well – it's falling over my eyes.
b This dress won't .... you at all. The colours are too bright. Choose something more sensible.

10 **bring take**
a Please .... all your rubbish away with you.
b Tom and Sally will .... their new baby to our house tomorrow.

11 **remind remember**
a I can't .... what time the meeting is.
b Can you .... me what happened at the meeting?

12 **price prize**
a Anne won first .... in the competition.
b I can give you a 10% discount on the ....

13 **borrow lend**
a Do you think we can .... the money from a bank?
b I never .... books to people.

14 **near nearby**
a My sister lives quite .... me.
b My house is next to the church and there is a small park ....

15 **raised rose**
a The student who knew the answer .... her hand.
b The river .... to danger level.

unit 6
HOW THINGS WORK

1 You are going to read a magazine article about white-water canoeing. Choose the most suitable heading from the list A–H for each part (1–7) of the article. There is one extra heading which you do not need to use.

A	Why do people do it?	E	What are the dangers?
B	What do you need to do it?	F	Where can you do it?
C	What is it?	G	How can you learn to do it?
D	Who are the champions?	H	Who does it?

White-water canoeing

1

White-water canoeing most often takes the form of a time trial between two points on a river. This can be a straight race, like downhill skiing or a slalom, in which the aim is to steer between two poles hanging from the ropes tied across the river. It can also, of course, be purely recreational.

2

You can canoe on most rivers, lakes and canals, but good fast-running white water is difficult to find. Scotland has numerous popular rivers and Wales is also very popular for canoeing.

3

Canoe, paddle, helmet, buoyancy (thin version of a life-jacket). A wet suit, cagoule and thermal clothes are also worth getting.

4

Canoeing appeals to people of all ages – there are rivers to suit a five-year-old novice and others strictly for the experienced canoeist. Rivers are graded one to six, like ski runs: one represents a canal, six a steep and dangerous rapid. Extreme canoeists search for dangerous rivers in mid-winter, when the water is highest.

5

'Canoeing is fantastic for anyone who likes adventure, getting away from the troubles of the city and into the wild outdoors,' says Cynthia Berry, one of Britain's top canoeists. 'It is never boring because the river or the weather is always changing. You can just potter about on a quiet river with your picnic packed in your canoe, or search out inhospitable and inaccessible rivers to find a real challenge.'

6

There are many disciplines – racing, slalom, rodeo – so it is difficult to say who is the best. It's rather like choosing the best skier. Cynthia Berry, 29, is ranked eighth in the world. She says a top canoeist needs good technique, concentration, observation and anticipation. It is vital to be a strong swimmer and many clubs insist new members take a life-saving qualification.

7

The obvious risks are drowning and striking rocks. One or two experienced canoeists are killed each year, but it is the untrained novice who has the highest chance of having an accident. Backs, shoulders and wrists suffer intense strain.

2 Read the text below. Use the word given in capitals at the end of each line to form a word that fits in the space in the same line. There is an example at the beginning (0).

New ways to make paper

It is common (0) ...knowledge... that paper is made from wood   **KNOW**

but there are other, rather unusual, (1) .... that can be used to   **PRODUCE**

manufacture paper. Using wood is not environmentally (2) ....   **FRIEND**

To bring about a (3) .... in the number of trees cut down, old   **REDUCE**

paper can be recycled and new paper can be used less (4) ....   **WASTE**

A (5) .... way is to make paper from beans, wheat and other   **THREE**

foodstuffs, even old tea leaves, which are easily (6) .... The   **RENEW**

problem is that this paper does not have the (7) .... necessary   **SMOOTH**

for printing but it is good enough for (8) .... and many other uses.   **WRAP**

Unfortunately, such paper is expensive but as consumer (9) ....   **AWARE**

increases, the price (and also the worldwide (10) .... of wood   **CONSUME**

pulp paper) should come down. You can't eat it, of course.

unit 6 HOW THINGS WORK

3 Read the text below and decide which answer (A, B, C or D) best fits each space. Put a circle round the letter that you choose. The exercise begins with an example (0).

Inventors and Inventions

An inventor is someone who discovers or produces a useful object or (0) .... that did not exist before. Many inventions enable people to do (1) .... they could not do before; others help them to work more (2) .... Some inventions, like the telephone or television, have had a (3) .... effect on the way people live. But (4) .... others may seem less revolutionary, they have had equally important (5) .... For example, the invention of the harness for horses changed the (6) .... of history because it allowed people to use horses for long journeys and to (7) .... heavy loads.

Many inventions have taken several centuries to develop into their modern (8) .... , so it is impossible to give a precise date for their creation. The history of the invention of the piano, for example, (9) .... more than 2,000 years. Experts have calculated that more than two thousand separate inventions and developments have contributed to the (10) .... of modern pianos.

When an inventor produces a new device, he or she usually (11) .... for a patent. This is a (12) .... which gives the inventor the exclusive (13) .... to make or sell the invention. Some people died rich and famous, having made a (14) .... from selling their inventions. Others died in poverty, (15) .... for their achievements.

0	(A) process	B method	C means	D idea
1	A actions	B things	C works	D anything
2	A carefully	B hardly	C efficiently	D mechanically
3	A strong	B large	C modern	D dramatic
4	A while	B as	C providing	D nevertheless
5	A developments	B consequences	C tendencies	D happenings
6	A story	B events	C course	D records
7	A pull	B make	C lift	D bring
8	A models	B machines	C uses	D forms
9	A is	B runs	C plays	D lasts
10	A type	B technique	C construction	D working
11	A applies	B enquires	C makes	D calls
12	A paper	B document	C mark	D register
13	A ownership	B permission	C claim	D right
14	A treasure	B fortune	C company	D living
15	A infamous	B rejected	C ignored	D unrecognised

4
Complete the second sentence so that it has a similar meaning to the first sentence. Use the word given and other words to complete each sentence. You must use between two and five words. Do not change the word given.

1 Does anyone know how to operate this machine?
   who
   Is .... how to operate this machine?

2 Arthur suddenly began to laugh before I finished telling the joke.
   burst
   Arthur .... before I finished telling the joke.

3 All their possessions were destroyed in the fire.
   everything
   They .... in the fire.

4 Have you nothing to say about this incident?
   anything
   Isn't .... want to say about this incident?

5 This part of the house needs redecorating.
   to
   This part of the house .... redecorated.

6 When the police arrived, there was nobody to be seen.
   see
   When the police arrived, ... anybody.

7 'I was the one who stole the documents,' said Bernard.
   stealing
   Bernard .... the documents.

8 We very much appreciate all the help you gave us.
   grateful
   We .... all the help you gave us.

9 Be extremely careful when you cross the glacier.
   risks
   Don't .... when crossing the glacier.

10 I'm sorry to disturb you but there's a telephone call for you.
   apologise
   I .... you but there's a telephone call for you.

5
Complete the sentences with a phrasal verb based on *look*.

EXAMPLE: I didn't know how to spell the word so I _looked_ it _up_ in the dictionary.

1 The city was full of interesting things to ....

2 I've .... everywhere .... my passport but can't find it.

3 The Prime Minister said he was going to .... the allegations that had been made.

4 No one .... from their work when the secretary entered the room.

5 People were stunned by the accident and just .... as the injured were taken away.

6 .... ! That lorry is going to overtake.

7 Jane hates watching violence and .... whenever anything unpleasant comes up on the TV screen.

8 If you ever come to London, you must .... us ....

9 We have two bedrooms, both of which .... the garden.

10 Mark .... people he thinks are inferior to him.

unit 1 THE FAMILY

1 You are going to read an article about the relationship between a father and his son. For questions 1–10, choose the answer (A, B, C or D) which you think fits best according to the text.

Home Life

Mark Emblem is a painter and works as a home decorator. His son Max, 15, is at school. They live in south-east London.

Rules and the odd row are part of life in a tiny flat.

On the floor of the kitchen there is a vase of dying flowers; two cats on a chair; the table is a clutter of papers, magazines, a bottle of wine and one of Tango orange drink. Sitting across the table from Mark, Max considers life with Dad.

'I was splitting my week between Mum and Dad, but it seemed a good idea to be based in one place. I have a bigger room in Mark's flat, so that's why I chose to live with him… It's important, because I spend a lot of time in my room – hanging out with friends, listening to music.'

Mark is listening, amused: 'We split up early in Max's life. Sarah, his mum, also thought it might be good for him, coming into adolescence, to live with me. I looked after Max quite a lot when he was very small, but of course this is different. I'd lived on my own for years, so I had to adjust to Max being here all the time. Sometimes it's frustrating. It's a tiny flat and we're both very territorial, so we've got clear rules about our own space.'

Max breaks in: 'But Mark doesn't realise how nosey he is with me. He's always knocking on the door, wanting to know what I'm doing. I don't want him coming in when I've got friends here. I like being left on my own.' And he looks sideways at Mark, slightly anxious he may have said too much.

Mark is listening carefully, not annoyed but intrigued, he says, because he and Max are not great ones for talking out their feelings – although their affection for each other is evident. He says: 'There's 20-odd years between us, so it is interesting, watching Max's life… But it makes me feel an outsider, very aware of my age.'

Mark's parents both died when he was in his mid-teens and he is very aware that he has no model from his own family life of how parents and adolescents cope with each other. He says: 'I've had to think about what's important, and for me it's that we're friends and trust each other, and I do feel we have that. There are times when we get very angry with each other and we both take this terribly male stance. We don't fight physically, but there's a lot of aggression. I don't feel proud of it, but there's a curious release in it, so long as it doesn't happen too often.'

What sets them against each other? Max wonders whether Mark isn't tougher as a single parent than he would be if he were still married: 'He gets at me for not telling him when I'm coming in; not phoning, but he does the same thing to me. He doesn't come back on time, doesn't phone, then when he comes in and I'm cross, he makes a joke of it.'

Mark has just started a BA in Fine Art at Goldsmith's College and there's not much money about. This doesn't worry him, but he's aware that being well off is something Max has in mind. His son nods emphatically: 'The way I feel at the moment I'd like to leave school quite soon and start working.' Meanwhile he is supplementing his pocket money by redecorating the flat – a trade he learned from Mark, who does painting and decorating to fund his studies.

The close moments are going to Clapham to play football – although they don't go to matches together as Mark hoped they would: 'I had visions of father-son bonding as we shared excitement over a goal. But Max is very much his own person. It's been good for me to learn to let him be that. And I'm pleased with him. I won't say proud, because it's not my word, but definitely pleased.'

Max pulls a face then unexpectedly gives the sweetest smile, and, in answer to the question: 'Are you proud of your Dad?' nods emphatically.

1 For Max, the advantage of living with his father is that
   A he is free to do whatever he wants.
   B he finds it easier to be with friends.
   C the flat is bigger than where he used to live.
   D music can be played anywhere in the flat.

2 When Max moved in, Mark
   A was forced to change his habits.
   B thought about life when he was young.
   C found it easy to adapt.
   D wished he would return to his mother.

3 'territorial' (line 21) means
   A wanting more space.
   B defending the area that belongs to you.
   C taking good care of what is yours.
   D being happy in a small space.

4 Max thinks that his father
   A is too curious about what he is doing.
   B is aggressive in his behaviour.
   C wants to share his social life.
   D shows him little affection.

5 Mark had some difficulty in knowing how to treat his son because
   A they had not been in touch for many years.
   B Max was used to his mother's ways.
   C Mark had no experience of that type of relationship.
   D Max behaved in a way he hadn't expected.

6 Because his father is a single parent, Max thinks Mark is
   A better able to put up with difficulties.
   B more bitter about life.
   C better able to resist pressure.
   D more likely to impose rules.

7 Where money is concerned,
   A Max wants to start earning as soon as possible.
   B father and son share the same attitude.
   C Mark worries about financing his studies.
   D father and son do odd jobs to bring in money.

8 'bonding' (line 70) means
   A preventing someone from moving.
   B establishing a committed relationship.
   C trying to stay close to someone.
   D treating someone like a slave.

9 Father and son like to spend time together
   A decorating the flat.
   B listening to music.
   C entertaining friends.
   D playing football.

10 Mark and Max consider that living together has
    A made them more critical of each other.
    B brought neither of them benefits.
    C helped their relationships with others.
    D deepened their understanding of each other.

2 Complete the sentences with the correct preposition.

EXAMPLE: Everyone was pleased __with__ their exam results.

1 She is famous .... writing books about her travels.

2 The customs officer was not satisfied .... my answer.

3 We are all tired .... eating the same thing for breakfast every day.

4 Are you ready .... the first race?

5 The team manager was confident .... success.

6 Please try not to be late .... dinner.

7 Many people are afraid .... the wild boars in this area.

8 Someone must be responsible .... locking the building at night.

9 This bag looks very similar .... mine.

10 This painting is typical .... Samuel Palmer's work.

SPEND! SPEND! SPEND!

When he was twenty-four, Martin Smith inherited one million pounds (0) __on__ the death of his grandmother. He had known (1) _____ several years that he (2) _____ inherit a large sum of money but he was surprised at (3) _____ large it turned out to be. His life (4) _____ been affected by the money even before he received it. After leaving university, at the age of twenty-one, he made (5) _____ serious attempt to start a career because he thought his inheritance would make (6) _____ unnecessary.

Martin began to enjoy a lavish lifestyle. He held extravagant parties and had (7) _____ of friends. 'But they were not true friends,' says Martin. They just wanted to help me spend my money. Sometimes I think people really (8) _____ advantage of me.' Once he bought a £5,000 stereo system. It was stolen from his flat the next day. He bought (9) _____ one and that was stolen too. 'I'm sure (10) _____ was giving information to the thieves,' says Martin.

In (11) _____ than two years Martin had spent (12) _____ the money and was in debt. He had to get a job in a supermarket to (13) _____ ends meet. He now accepts that he must work for his (14) _____ but has not given up his dreams of wealth. 'I bought a lottery ticket recently,' he said. 'If I won, I'd have a better idea (15) _____ to do with the money next time.'

4 Read the text below and look carefully at each line. Some of the lines are correct and some have a word which should not be there. Write the wrong word in the space provided and tick the correct lines. There are two examples at the beginning (0) and (00).

A Family Reunion

I am writing to ask you if you wouldn't mind if I came and   0 ✓

stayed with you for a few days. I am really need to get   00 am

away for a while. You have perhaps remember that I   1 ....

told you about my mother's idea of having a big family   2 ....

reunion. Well, it has finally happened. Nearly all our own   3 ....

relatives, not just from other parts of the United Kingdom   4 ....

but also them from Canada and Australia, are staying at our   5 ....

house which, as you know, it is quite big. Unfortunately, the   6 ....

reunion has not been such a happy one and I am not enjoying   7 ....

it. The house is become very crowded. Because people have   8 ....

come the long distances, they are staying for several weeks not   9 ....

just one or two days. There have been lots arguments nearly   10 ....

every day. People who have not met all for years do not   11 ....

want to speak to each other one ever again. Many 'skeletons   12 ....

in cupboards' have come out. I really can't stand it any   13 ....

longer. Can you phone to me soon, preferably early in the   14 ....

morning before everybody starts making up long distance   15 ....

phone calls?

Unit 8 GOOD COMPANIONS

1 You are going to read a newspaper article. Six sentences have been removed from the article. Fill each gap (1–6) with the sentence which you think fits best from the list A–G. There is one extra sentence which you do not need to use.

Thanks for the memory

PET CEMETERIES, STONE memorials or even proper funeral services for pets – these seem freaky and embarrassing. **1**____ So says agony aunt Virginia Ironside, whose book on pet bereavement, *Goodbye Dear Friend*, was published last week.

'I don't understand why people jeer,' she says. '**2**____ There are lots of pets buried in people's gardens.'

The aristocracy have often given their pets proper burials. The Queen buries her dogs in the gardens of royal houses and erects a gravestone for each one. Queen Victoria buried one pet dog at Windsor with a tombstone. **3**____ Lord Byron put up a monument for his Newfoundland dog, Boatswain, remembering him as one who 'possessed beauty without vanity, strength without insolence, courage without ferocity and all the virtues of a man without his vices'.

4____ Whenever Ironside mentions pet bereavement in her newspaper agony column, letters pour in from heart-broken readers telling her how gravestones, cemeteries and sometimes even keeping the ashes helped owners cope with loss. One family carried out a complete ceremony for their pet, Bobo. The funeral parlour provided a hearse and a cremation. **5**____ 'She told me she plans to dig it up and take it with her when she moves.' Lady Munnings, the eccentric wife of the painter, had her Pekinese dog stuffed after its death and took it everywhere, even to the Lord Mayor's dinner. Other suggestions for coping with the loss include making up a special book of photos, putting an obituary in a pet magazine, or writing memorial poetry. 'Many people have sent me poetry,' says Ironside. '**6**____ Writing a poem is a good way of expressing your feeling secretly.' After all, writing a poem about the death of a pet is following the example of writers as great as Byron, Wordsworth and Hardy.

A Ironside also heard from a woman who had buried her cat in a box in the garden.

B It seems to be flying in the face of convention to bury your pet, yet my impression is that it's on the increase.

C There is a pet cemetery in Hyde Park in London.

D If Royals and peers find comfort in putting up a memorial to their animals, why shouldn't other people?

E The Duke of Wellington's favourite horse, Copenhagen, from whose back he directed the Battle of Waterloo, was buried on his estate and given a headstone.

F The problem of mourning a pet is that if you tell somebody, you may get laughed at.

G Yet they may be a great comfort for those mourning a much-loved animal.

2 Read the text below. Use the word given in capitals at the end of each line to form a word that fits in the space in the same line. There is an example at the beginning (0).

Skiing

Many people get a lot of (0) __enjoyment__ from skiing. It   **ENJOY**

is popular as a leisure (1) _____ for people of all ages and also   **ACT**

as a highly (2) _____ sport which can be practised up to Olympic   **COMPETE**

standard. Nowadays, skiing is much less (3) _____ than it used   **RISK**

to be because of the (4) _____ bindings on skis. These release   **SAFE**

the skier's feet (5) _____ if he or she falls. In this way, the chance   **AUTOMATIC**

of a (6) _____ leg or torn muscle is greatly reduced. However,   **BREAK**

skiers must still beware of (7) _____ with other skiers on crowded slopes.   **COLLIDE**

The spectacular mountain (8) _____ , bright sunshine, fresh air and   **SCENE**

the sheer (9) _____ of moving at high speed attract thousands of   **EXCITE**

people to the (10) _____ mountainous regions of the world.   **SNOW**

unit 8 Good Companions

3 Read the text below and look carefully at each line. Some of the lines are correct and some have a word which should not be there. Write the wrong word in the space provided and tick the correct lines. There are two examples at the beginning (0) and (00).

Saved by a cat

A really extraordinary incident has happened in our house last week.	0	has
You remember that I told you that since last September, when I started	00	✓
college, I have been sharing out a house with three other students. We	1	
rent it quite cheaply but it is not in a good state of repair. Well, when we	2	
first moved into the house there was a cat which already there, probably	3	
left behind by the previous tenants. Nobody took very much notice of	4	
this cat but it wouldn't go away. We fed it but none of us wanted really	5	
looked after it. Anyway, one evening we were all watching at television	6	
and the cat, which was in the room, it got slowly to its feet and walked	7	
out, making the horrible coughing noises. I got up to see what was	8	
the matter with and suddenly felt very dizzy and unwell. I followed the	9	
cat out into the garden and felt much better than when I breathed	10	
fresh air. Then I made the other three to come outside too. They also	11	
felt unwell until they got outside into the garden. It turned out that our	12	
gas fire wasn't working properly and was giving lot off poisonous	13	
fumes. The cat, being small, was affected first. If I hadn't have followed	14	
it out, or if it hadn't been there at all, I might not be telling you this story.	15	

unit 8 GOOD COMPANIONS

4 Complete the second sentence so that it has a similar meaning to the first sentence. Use the word given and other words to complete each sentence. You must use between two and five words. Do not change the word given.

1 Why didn't you pay him what you owed?
   should
   You .... him what you owed.

2 Jack was sorry he had lied to Christine.
   lying
   Jack .... to Christine.

3 We discussed the plan for a long time.
   had
   We .... the plan.

4 The president has officially requested our help.
   for
   The president has .... our help.

5 Could you accompany me to the doctor's surgery?
   with
   I'd like you .... to the doctor's surgery.

6 For him to have run from here to the station in ten minutes is impossible.
   could
   He .... from here to the station in ten minutes.

7 You can eat as many cakes as you like.
   help
   Please .... as many cakes as you want.

8 Everybody was surprised by the end of the film, weren't they?
   like
   Nobody expected the film .... , ... they?

9 The police prevented the situation from getting out of control.
   under
   The police .... control.

10 When the athlete did not succeed in breaking the record he was very upset.
    to
    The .... break the record made him very upset.

5 Complete the sentences with a phrasal verb based on *come*.

EXAMPLE: We asked our visitors to ......*come in*...... out of the rain.

1 Mr Smith is on holiday this week but he .... on Monday.

2 If you explain everything to Jim, he'll .... your way of thinking.

3 The staff were sad to learn that sales figures .... by ten per cent.

4 Would you like to .... to our house tonight and have something to eat with us?

5 I enjoyed climbing up the mountain but it was more difficult to ....

6 Whenever Tom eats strawberries he .... in a rash.

7 Harry was knocked unconscious in the fight and only .... three hours later in hospital.

8 .... Sally! Everyone is waiting for you.

9 John left home last month and refuses to ....

10 When the new biography of the writer appears, the facts of the relationship will ....

37

unit 9 EMOTIONS AND FEELINGS

1 You are going to read a magazine article about married couples. For questions 1–14 choose from the people (A–F). Some of the people may be chosen more than once. When more than one answer is required, these may be given in any order.

Which person

was forced by education to spend time away from their partner?	1	
first met their partner in an educational institution?	2 .... 3	
never considered marrying anyone else?	4	
at first found it difficult to express their feelings?	5	
recognises differences in the relationship before and after marriage?	6	**A** ROSANGELA
		B CARLOS
used a special feature of the calendar to propose marriage?	7	**C** GABRIELLE
		D MIKE
recognises the value of time spent away from other family members?	8	**E** KIRPAL
		F HARBANS
recognises the relationship may change in the future?	9	
thinks their partner's looks have improved?	10	
had to leave someone else to be with their partner?	11 .... 12	
recognises character differences between self and partner?	13	
felt external forces were at work in the relationship?	14	

unit **9** EMOTIONS AND FEELINGS

CHILDHOOD SWEETHEARTS

Rosangela Masuzzo, 27, artist and designer, and Carlos De Lima, 27, marketing assistant

Rosangela: Carlos and I knew each other at school in Brazil when we were nine. I remember him sending me messages asking me to meet him. Then he moved away and I didn't see him again for over ten years. I went to Spain after that and then came to England. One day, I went to an art exhibition in London with my boyfriend, and there was Carlos, in the same room. The moment I saw him I realised he was my first love – it seemed too good to be true that we had met again, and we started talking. As we were both in other relationships at the time, we just became good friends for a couple of years. Then, two years ago, we realised we wanted to be together. I think we'll be together for ever now. I feel lucky to have found Carlos again.

Carlos: I remember once catching Rosangela's eye at primary school and thinking, 'Wow!' But I was very, very shy. I used to get my brother to deliver love notes to her. When I was eleven, I moved to another area, and years later I came to England. One day I went to an art exhibition in London and we found ourselves standing next to each other. I turned to her and it struck me that I knew her from somewhere. It was like destiny.

Gabrielle Bliss, 35, mother, and her husband, Mike, 38, designer and manufacturer of the range of Bliss lights and clocks

Gabrielle: It was love across the disco. I was fifteen, he was eighteen. I went up to him because he was looking lonely. We got on very well. After that, Mike used to cycle ten miles to see me. Then he went away to college, and I went to see him as often as I could. One day I suddenly said, 'It's a leap* year. Will you marry me?' He said, 'Yeah.' I consider Mike to be my best friend. But I'll never assume he'll always be there and never be attracted to someone else. There should always be that edge, I think.

Mike: We've got a business and a family now, but we're still as happy as we've ever been. We try to get away on our own quite a lot; it's important to spend time together and not to be enslaved to the kids. I've never thought I should have married someone else. I'm very laid back, while Gabrielle is a bit temperamental. We are quite volatile together sometimes, which makes things exciting within a long-lasting relationship.

Kirpal Ruprah, 63, retired shop owner, and her husband, Harbans, 70, President of the Overseas Indian Congress

Kirpal: I first saw Harbans near our house in Simla, India, in 1948. I liked him, but we didn't really talk. When my father showed me a few boys suitable for marriage, I didn't like any of them, so he said, 'If you have anybody in mind, tell me.' So then he went to visit Harban's family. Then we got engaged. I don't think it makes much difference if you know someone or not before you get married because the life you share after marriage is completely different from any relationship you might have beforehand. Tolerance is important: we let each other do what the other wants and we are happy.

Harbans: I couldn't think of getting to know my wife before we were married. We spoke to each other a little, in front of relatives but never alone. The first time I was alone with her was after we were married. Today my wife is more beautiful to me than she was when we married 43 years ago. We don't argue – we co-operate with each other – that's one reason why we are happy.

*a leap year: a year with 366 days

unit 9 EMOTIONS AND FEELINGS

2 Read the text below and think of the word which best fits each space. Use only one word in each space. There is an example at the beginning (0).

Regrets? I've had a few

What do people most regret about (0) ...**their**... lives? Is it the mistakes they made which they (1) .... they hadn't? Or is it the things they didn't (2) .... which cause the most regret? Recent research shows that people feel a much stronger (3) .... of regret about missed opportunities. They regret not training (4) .... a career, not learning a skill, not emigrating to (5) .... country and not developing personal relationships, even when they had the opportunity to do (6) .... People don't feel regret at situations (7) .... their control. It is situations in which they (8) .... have acted but failed to act that give rise to regret.

Obviously, people have more regrets (9) .... they get older. Interviews with middle-aged men and women indicate some differences (10) .... the sexes. Women tend to regret marrying too young and not taking advantage of educational opportunities. Men tend to regret not spending (11) .... time with their families when their children were small. Almost (12) .... expresses regret (13) .... not having the courage to take a risk. They regret (14) .... too careful and too cautious. What can young people learn from these experiences? Undoubtedly, that the Latin saying *carpe diem* ('seize the day') is one to be (15) .... seriously.

3 Complete the second sentence so that it has a similar meaning to the first sentence. Use the word given and other words to complete each sentence. You must use between two and five words. Do not change the word given.

1 Robin was surprised that he was unable to hit the target.
his
Robin was surprised .... to hit the target.

2 If you work for that company, you can gain a lot of experience.
opportunity
Working for that company will .... to gain a lot of experience.

3 We were all amazed when the manager suddenly left.
departure
The .... the manager amazed us all.

4 The baby weighed three kilos when it was born.
in
The baby was .... at birth.

5 It was obvious that the runners were exhausted by the end of the race.
was
By the end of the race, the .... obvious.

6 All the vegetables we eat come from our own garden.
grow
We .... vegetables in our garden.

7 Is Guy telling the truth?
says
Is .... true?

8 Despite many interruptions, the minister finished his speech.
times
Although .... , the minister finished his speech.

9 We were all surprised when the train arrived ahead of schedule.
early
The .... the train surprised us all.

10 Don't let me forget this afternoon's appointment.
of
Be sure .... this afternoon's appointment.

4 Complete the sentences with a phrasal verb based on *break*.

EXAMPLE: Someone ___broke into___ the headquarters of the political party and stole some important documents.

1 Three prisoners .... of the prison yesterday and have still not been recaptured.

2 A dispute .... between the two sides as to what should happen.

3 Caroline and Martin have decided to .... their engagement.

4 My parents' marriage .... when I was four years old and I went to live with my father.

5 There's a time in everyone's life when they need to .... from their parents.

6 When war .... , many people tried to leave the country.

7 I took out insurance in case the car .... on the long journey to the coast.

8 The ship was blown onto the rocks and .... after three days in heavy seas.

9 The government threatened to .... relations with the country that they thought offered a refuge for terrorists.

10 They decided to .... tradition and got married on a beach.

unit 10
MAKING THE MOST OF YOURSELF

1 You are going to read a magazine article about fitness. For questions 1–17, choose from the list of clubs (A–F). Some of the clubs may be used more than once. When more than one answer is required, these may be given in any order.

Which of the clubs		
makes users undergo training before they can use the equipment?	1	
charges extra for special facilities?	2	
has no pool?	3 .... 4	
shares a building with a theatre?	5	
has overcome the danger of closure?	6	
has changed the kind of sports activities on offer?	7	**A** Academy Health and Fitness Centre
is considered the best by the writer of the article?	8	**B** Archway Pool and Leisure Centre
has somewhere for clients to eat?	9 .... 10	**C** Champneys, The London Club
makes special arrangements for those who have previously consulted a doctor?	11	**D** Drill Hall Arts Centre
runs a training programme for fitness trainers?	12	**E** Lingfield Health Club
has an expensively decorated pool?	13	**F** London Central YMCA
has times when it may only be used by people of one sex?	14	
makes use of up-to-date equipment in assessing people's fitness?	15	
was previously used for educational purposes?	16	
made the existing gym bigger?	17	

42

unit **10** MAKING THE MOST OF YOURSELF

THE TIME OUT GUIDE TO FITNESS

Last year a Department of Health survey of more than 3000 adults across Britain produced disturbing results. Fewer than one in eight men, and one in nine women, are free of all the risk factors which can cause a heart attack or stroke. Only one in five men, and one in eight women, take enough rigorous exercise to protect against heart disease.

Londoners will always claim a shortage of time as the reason for their inactivity, but they can't claim a shortage of facilities. The capital has more than 100 public swimming pools and more than 200 sports centres. There are also dozens of private health and fitness clubs. Here are six of the best.

Academy Health and Fitness Centre

Located in a converted school building, which had been empty for 25 years, the Academy is a club which specialises in the martial arts but also offers a full programme of exercise classes, a well-equipped gym, and a pleasant cafe. Plants and pine set the tone, which is enhanced by knowledgeable and friendly staff.

Archway Pool and Leisure Centre

The Archway has recently upgraded its facilities, adding a sauna and a splendid new gym with 20 multi-station exercise units and satellite TV. The aim is to provide a friendly facility rather than a weight-trainer's gym, working with people who want to tone up rather than build bulky muscle. All users must complete an induction course, which costs £5, and computerised fitness testing is now available. A free swim is included in the price of your workout. Perhaps the most interesting development at this busy centre is a partnership with Camden and Islington Health Authority, which will allow anyone with fitness problems to obtain a doctor's prescription giving them use of the facilities at preferential rates.

Champneys, The London Club

The club is spread over an acre of Piccadilly, with Romanesque-style decor if you like that kind of thing. There's no questioning the facilities, though: the pool, with its marble surround, is the centre-piece, and there are two squash courts; two saunas, steam room and spa bath; an aerobics studio; five beauty treatment rooms – apparently used more by men than women; and an elegant drawing room and restaurant.

Drill Hall Arts Centre

Though perhaps best known as a theatre venue, the Drill Hall also runs an extensive and affordable fitness programme. For example, Jenny Whitby's popular 'Below the Belt' conditioning classes are held three times a week; there are several step, aerobics and stretch workouts; and you can even try acrobatics or one of the dance classes. All are open to both sexes, except sessions held on Mondays, when the Drill Hall is women-only, and you pay for what you do – there's no membership fee.

Lingfield Health Club

Lingfield clubs were big on squash when that sport was the fashionable way to keep fit. Now that that fad has passed, the group has been busy adapting its facilities to suit today's more measured approach to fitness. That means an expanded gym, aerobics studio with a wide range of classes, small pool, therapy rooms and an atmosphere of gentle enthusiasm. The building itself used to be two large houses, so the rooms are all differently-shaped – a pleasing alternative to the straight lines and angles of most new-built clubs. Membership fees are reasonable for the area, and the off-peak rate is something of a bargain.

London Central YMCA

Questions were asked in parliament when the 'Y' seemed in danger of closing last year, but the future of the best facility in town is now secure. Many join just to use the 25m pool, which is an inviting deep blue and divided into separate lanes for serious swimmers and those who just wish to splash; but the gym is comprehensive, you can try sports including trampolining, volleyball and basketball, and the classes are superb – as they should be, for the Y's Training and Development Department sets many of the standards for the teaching of fitness instructors. Membership fees depend on your age, and the only extra charges are to use the sunbeds and sauna.

unit 10 MAKING THE MOST OF YOURSELF

2 Read the text below and decide which answer (A, B, C or D) best fits each space. Put a circle round the letter that you choose. The exercise begins with an example (0).

INTERPRETING

Interpreting at (0) .... international conferences is an extremely demanding job which requires a variety of abilities. As well as a thorough knowledge of at (1) .... two languages, interpreters must have a wide range of (2) .... and be able to concentrate (3) .... They also need a good general knowledge of how their own society (4) .... 'When interpreters fail to (5) .... the highest ranks of the profession,' says the head of a (6) .... agency, 'it is not because they lack expertise in the foreign language. Many would-be interpreters have (7) .... years in a foreign country, have travelled (8) .... in it and have a first-rate understanding of its culture. The problem is that they don't know enough about their own country. They may not have visited (9) .... of it and have only a limited knowledge of its economy, politics and business (10) .... In some (11) .... , their vocabulary and knowledge of idiomatic expressions may be greater in the foreign language than in their own.'

Even if an interpreter (12) .... work, it can be difficult to develop a career. For an important conference only the very best interpreters will be employed because everything must run (13) .... and there can be no (14) .... for error. This can make it difficult for younger interpreters to (15) .... the experience they need to become the best.

0	A	principle	B	top (circled)	C	primary	D	main
1	A	best	B	once	C	least	D	first
2	A	interests	B	specialities	C	topics	D	ideas
3	A	strongly	B	hardly	C	deeply	D	intensively
4	A	goes	B	works	C	runs	D	acts
5	A	take	B	catch	C	reach	D	hold
6	A	leading	B	directing	C	winning	D	selecting
7	A	taken	B	known	C	spent	D	gone
8	A	broadly	B	widely	C	deeply	D	lengthily
9	A	anything	B	places	C	everything	D	much
10	A	ways	B	practices	C	manner	D	system
11	A	approaches	B	areas	C	parts	D	studies
12	A	offers	B	makes	C	does	D	obtains
13	A	currently	B	comprehensively	C	finely	D	smoothly
14	A	room	B	space	C	opportunity	D	chance
15	A	gain	B	seek	C	receive	D	meet

ANSWERS

unit 1 PEOPLE AND CLOTHES

1
1 B
2 F
3 I
4 G
5 D
6 A
7 C

2
1 wearing, carrying
2 wear
3 put on
4 carry
5 carry
6 wear
7 put on
8 worn
9 take off
10 wear

3
1 suit
2 matched
3 suit
4 matching, fitted
5 suits
6 suits
7 matched
8 fit
9 suit
10 match

4
1 long showerproof
2 shabby old
3 shiny waist-length
4 waterproof rubber
5 expensive designer
6 cool cotton
7 tight black
8 pretty new
9 green check/baggy brown
10 creased linen

5
1 become
2 were
3 doing
4 with
5 while/when
6 which
7 from
8 where
9 against/from
10 likely
11 could, would, might
12 as
13 their
14 because, since, as
15 all

6
1 to
2 for
3 ✓
4 the
5 at
6 himself
7 their
8 all
9 would
10 ✓
11 ✓
12 out
13 being
14 ✓
15 too

unit 2 A PLACE OF YOUR OWN

1
1 B
2 A
3 D
4 C
5 B
6 C
7/8 A,D
9/10 C,D
11 B
12/13 A,D
14 B
15 B
16 A

2
1 B
2 A
3 D
4 A
5 B
6 D
7 A
8 C
9 A
10 B
11 A
12 D
13 A
14 B
15 A

3
1 is the first time
2 matter which (one) you
3 going there by myself
4 since this/the dog was (last)
5 are responsible for cleaning
6 can't/cannot buy a better/can buy no better
7 how you felt
8 can hardly see
9 had/raised no objection(s)
10 (to have) a word

4
1 a Who won a prize for her first novel?
  b What did Margaret win (a prize for)?
2 a Who started the meeting?
  b When did the meeting start?/When did Mr Thomas start the meeting?
3 a What crashed into the sea?
  b Where did the rocket crash?
4 a How many people bought lottery tickets?
  b What did thousands of people buy?
5 a Who spent three years in prison?
  b How long did Martin spend in prison?
6 a Who cooked us plenty of food?
  b How much food did Mrs Jones cook (us)?
7 a Who met many interesting people?
  b Where did Simon meet many interesting people?
8 a Who cancelled the race?
  b Why did the manager cancel the race?

unit 3 MAKING A NEW START

1
1/2 B,H
3 D
4 E
5 B
6/7 A,H
8 G
9 F
10 C
11 E
12 F
13 H
14/15 A,C

ANSWERS

2
1. ✓
2. to
3. any
4. soon
5. ✓
6. with
7. of
8. ✓
9. the
10. am
11. that
12. rather
13. live
14. real
15. might

3
1. gave birth to
2. to have a go
3. necessary (for us) to
4. go (back)/return home by
5. you don't leave
6. apologise for not warning/for failing to warn
7. had better pay
8. make (the) arrangements for
9. made no decision/not made any decision/a decision
10. the determination shown/displayed by

4
1. went on
2. went out
3. go away
4. went up
5. went out
6. go off
7. goes down
8. go for
9. went off
10. go into

unit 4 GETTING ABOUT

1
1. A
2. B
3/4. B,D
5/6. C,D
7. F
8. G
9/10. A,D
11. C
12. E
13. A
14. D

2
1. Instead/First/Firstly
2. that
3. through
4. will
5. what
6. with
7. our/my
8. through/into
9. somewhere
10. over
11. any
12. let
13. no
14. my
15. again

3
1. didn't expect so many
2. give me some help (in/with)
3. has no intention of commenting
4. in charge of
5. at/by his refusal
6. no regrets about
7. up (all) hope of finding
8. plenty of encouragement
9. have the owner's permission/the permission of the owner
10. you received an/your invitation to

4
1. keep out
2. keep up
3. keep … from
4. keeps on
5. keep up
6. keep to
7. keep to
8. keep away
9. kept in
10. keep … up

unit 5 CAKES AND ALE

1
1. C
2. E
3. A
4. F
5. D
6. H
7. B

2
1. known
2. mice
3. heavily
4. combinations
5. rotten
6. addition
7. management
8. revisions
9. appearances
10. advice

3
1. B
2. D
3. A
4. D
5. B
6. C
7. A
8. C
9. A
10. D
11. D
12. C
13. B
14. B
15. D

4
1. a permit — b permission
2. a despite — b although
3. a checked — b controlled
4. a interesting — b profitable
5. a marks — b notes
6. a injured — b wounded
7. a sensitive — b sensible
8. a advice — b advise
9. a fit — b suit
10. a take — b bring
11. a remember — b remind
12. a prize — b price
13. a borrow — b lend
14. a near — b nearby
15. a raised — b rose

2

ANSWERS

unit 6 HOW THINGS WORK

1
1 C
2 F
3 B
4 H
5 A
6 D
7 E

2
1 products
2 friendly
3 reduction
4 wastefully
5 third
6 renewable
7 smoothness
8 wrapping
9 awareness
10 consumption

3
1 B
2 C
3 D
4 A
5 B
6 C
7 A
8 D
9 D
10 C
11 A
12 B
13 D
14 B
15 D

4
1 there anyone who knows
2 burst out laughing
3 lost everything (they owned)
4 there anything you
5 needs to be
6 they couldn't see
7 admitted stealing/confessed to stealing
8 are (very) grateful for
9 take any risks
10 apologise for disturbing

5
1 look at
2 looked … for
3 look into
4 looked up
5 looked on
6 Look out
7 looks away
8 look … up
9 look onto
10 looks down on

unit 7 THE FAMILY

1
1 B
2 A
3 B
4 A
5 C
6 D
7 A
8 B
9 D
10 D

2
1 for
2 with
3 of
4 for
5 of
6 for
7 of
8 for
9 to
10 of

3
1 for
2 would
3 how
4 had
5 no
6 that, it, this
7 lots, plenty
8 took
9 another
10 someone, somebody
11 less
12 all
13 make
14 living
15 what

4
1 have
2 ✓
3 own
4 ✓
5 them
6 it
7 ✓
8 become
9 the
10 lots
11 all
12 one
13 ✓
14 to
15 up

unit 8 GOOD COMPANIONS

1
1 G
2 B
3 E
4 D
5 A
6 F

2
1 activity
2 competitive
3 risky
4 safety
5 automatically
6 broken
7 collisions/colliding
8 scenery
9 excitement
10 snowy

3
1 out
2 ✓
3 which
4 ✓
5 wanted
6 at
7 it
8 the
9 with
10 than
11 to
12 ✓
13 lot
14 have
15 ✓

4
1 should have paid
2 regretted lying
3 had a long discussion/long discussions about
4 made an official request for
5 to come/go with me
6 could not have run

3

ANSWERS

7 help yourself/yourselves to
8 to end like that/would end like that, did
9 kept the situation under
10 athlete's failure to/failure of the athlete to

5 1 is coming back
   2 come round to
   3 had come down
   4 come round
   5 come down
   6 comes out
   7 came round
   8 Come on
   9 come back
   10 come out

unit 9 EMOTIONS AND FEELINGS

1 1 D
   2/3 A,B
   4 D
   5 B
   6 E
   7 C
   8 D
   9 C
   10 F
   11/12 A,B
   13 D
   14 B

2 1 wish
   2 do
   3 sense
   4 for
   5 another
   6 so
   7 beyond/outside
   8 could
   9 as/when
   10 between
   11 enough
   12 everybody, everyone
   13 at
   14 being
   15 taken

3 1 at his inability/failure
   2 will give you the/an opportunity
   3 sudden departure of
   4 three kilos in weight
   5 exhaustion of the runners/ runners' exhaustion was
   6 grow all our own
   7 what Guy says
   8 he was interrupted many times
   9 early arrival of
   10 to remind me of

4 1 broke out
   2 broke out
   3 break off
   4 broke up
   5 break away
   6 broke out
   7 broke down
   8 broke up
   9 break off
   10 break with

unit 10 MAKING THE MOST OF YOURSELF

1 1 B
   2 F
   3/4 A,D
   5 D
   6 F
   7 E
   8 F
   9/10 A,C
   11 B
   12 F
   13 C
   14 D
   15 B
   16 A
   17 E

2 1 C
   2 A
   3 D
   4 B
   5 C
   6 A
   7 C
   8 B
   9 D
   10 B
   11 B
   12 D
   13 D
   14 A
   15 A

3 1 technological
   2 possibility
   3 further, farther
   4 forgotten
   5 ridiculous
   6 designer
   7 operation
   8 assistance
   9 moving
   10 driven

unit 11 THINGS THAT GO WRONG

1 1 B
   2 H
   3 E
   4 C
   5 I
   6 A
   7 D
   8 F

2 1 might have been stolen
   2 must have been destroyed
   3 could have been killed
   4 has not been discovered
   5 had been signed
   6 has been injured
   7 have been interviewed
   8 is cleaned
   9 are being analysed
   10 was founded
   11 will have been sent/will be sent
   12 will be sold
   13 should not have been given
   14 to be checked

4

3
1 no
2 as
3 able
4 far
5 nowhere
6 had
7 himself
8 neither
9 could
10 too
11 chance
12 which
13 what
14 will
15 from

4
1 animal's unusual behaviour was
2 the most frightening
3 your plans for the
4 haven't been any complaints
5 an explanation for
6 had made a speech
7 would do anything
8 changed her mind about going
9 always remember his first visit
10 had difficulty (in) understanding

5
1 pulled out
2 pull off
3 pulled in to
4 pulled out
5 pulled ahead
6 pulled down
7 pull out
8 pull over
9 pull through
10 to pull apart

unit 12 WEATHER AND CLIMATE

1
1 B
2 C
3 B
4 B
5 C
6 B

2
1 but
2 so as not to
3 so that
4 By the time
5 as if
6 so
7 Although
8 Just as
9 despite
10 in which
11 as long as
12 because of
13 whose
14 in case
15 because

3
1 C
2 A
3 C
4 A
5 B
6 D
7 D
8 A
9 B
10 A
11 D
12 C
13 B
14 A
15 D

4
1 ✓
2 on
3 themselves
4 out
5 ✓
6 do
7 an
8 ✓
9 such
10 at
11 most
12 of
13 as
14 some
15 to

unit 13 HEROES AND HEROINES?

1
1 C
2/3 D,E
4/5 B,C
6 A
7 A
8 D
9 E
10 B
11 A
12/13 B,C
14 D
15 D
16 C

2
1 an
2 which
3 as
4 it
5 was
6 although
7 later
8 would
9 set
10 where
11 out
12 when
13 at
14 number
15 mainly, mostly, especially

3
1 prevented/kept him from opening
2 to get over
3 have no difficulty (in) translating
4 is a friend of mine
5 surprised by the sudden change
6 popularity increased/grew with
7 is not as healthy as
8 injuries were so serious
9 revealed her reluctance
10 made a swift recovery

4
1 pushed through
2 pushed ... back
3 push ... in
4 push ... off/over
5 pushed up
6 pushed off
7 push on
8 pushed down

ANSWERS

unit 14 VICTIMS AND VILLAINS

1
1 C
2 G
3 A
4 F
5 B
6 E

2
1 on
2 on
3 on
4 in
5 from
6 in
7 to
8 for
9 in
10 on

3
1 borrow
2 lenders
3 borrowed
4 lend
5 borrow
6 lend
7 borrowed
8 lent
9 borrowed
10 Borrowing

4
1 A
2 B
3 A
4 B
5 D
6 A
7 C
8 A
9 A
10 B
11 C
12 D
13 D
14 C
15 B

5
1 told us a lie
2 his great disappointment
3 arrangements for my journey were
4 at Sybille's decision
5 is no need/necessity
6 excitement of the spectators grew/rose/increased
7 showed (absolutely) no interest (at all)
8 caused/created great alarm
9 are worried about their son's
10 were given wrong/incorrect information by

6
1 turn down
2 turn up
3 turned down
4 turned out
5 turned over
6 turn in
7 turned out
8 turn back
9 turned (a)round
10 turned off

unit 15 LIES, TRICKS AND DECEIT

1
1 C
2 A
3 G
4 B
5 F
6 D

2
1 action
2 collisions
3 reliable
4 movements
5 activity
6 location
7 observers
8 equipment
9 measurements
10 illumination

3
1 out
2 us
3 had
4 being
5 of
6 ✓
7 in
8 as
9 the
10 ✓
11 so
12 what
13 ✓
14 an
15 times

4
1 Martin (very much) enjoyed looking after his pet snake (very much).
2 The news was far worse than I expected.
3 Don't sunbathe for more than thirty minutes.
4 You will have to work hard until you finish.
5 After the storm, we could see that the damage was not serious.
6 My new office is near my house so I won't spend a lot of money on the journey to work.
7 I have always liked nature.
8 John has succeeded in getting a better job.
9 Like my father, I love playing golf.
10 Sally is quite an intelligent child.
11 Nowadays, most people have a car.
12 Jack speaks Greek fluently.
13 I like visiting art galleries.
14 Sarah flies to the United States tomorrow.
15 In this part of the country, it is usually very cold most of the year.
16 My favourite subject is economics.
17 They arrived in Edinburgh three weeks ago.
18 My grandfather would not agree to show me the letters.
19 Tom advised me not to go to the exhibition.
20 I will buy the book as soon as I go into town.

unit 16 A THING OF BEAUTY IS A JOY FOREVER

1
1 E
2 B
3 H
4 A
5 F
6 G
7 D

2
1 thought
2 location
3 security
4 inaccessible
5 astonishment
6 alive/living
7 significant
8 survival
9 height
10 popularity

3
1 C
2 A
3 B
4 C
5 A
6 D
7 D
8 B
9 A
10 B
11 C
12 C
13 D
14 B
15 D

4
1 mention tomorrow's
2 suggested delivering/(that) we should deliver
3 of tennis practice
4 resentment at
5 used to (operating/using/working with)
6 would like to know
7 were new players chosen by
8 needs to be wound up/winding up
9 is a possibility
10 pointless asking/to ask

5
1 say, told
2 tell
3 say
4 speak
5 talk
6 say
7 tells
8 speak
9 talking, says
10 spoken

unit 17 A SENSE OF ACHIEVEMENT

1
1 C
2 F
3 B
4 D
5 H
6 A
7 G

2
1 collect
2 bring
3 collected
4 took
5 brought
6 take
7 take
8 take
9 bring
10 collecting

3
1 still
2 yet
3 still
4 still
5 yet
6 already
7 still
8 still
9 already, yet
10 already
11 already, still
12 already

4
1 about
2 by
3 about
4 to
5 of
6 of
7 on
8 of
9 of
10 with

5
1 out/behind
2 when/if/whenever
3 who
4 any
5 since
6 in
7 better
8 what
9 comes
10 would
11 their
12 off
13 make
14 all/many
15 may/will/might/should

6
1 ✓
2 first
3 as
4 with
5 ✓
6 it
7 me
8 the
9 ✓
10 a
11 ✓
12 which
13 for
14 doing
15 be

unit 18 TIME AFTER TIME

1
1 A
2 C
3 C
4 C
5 D
6 B
7 B
8 D

2
1 not to enter
2 signing
3 getting
4 to pick up
5 buying
6 to lift
7 growing
8 driving
9 to live
10 to lock
11 studying
12 digging
13 to inform

7

ANSWERS

3   1 ✓
    2 year
    3 total
    4 ✓
    5 of
    6 ✓
    7 away
    8 back
    9 the
    10 you
    11 be
    12 ✓
    13 being
    14 those
    15 ✓

4   1 on condition (that) you promise
    2 made no attempt/effort
    3 instructions did you give (to)
    4 got to the end of
    5 denied signing/that he had signed
    6 we should have bought
    7 has been to prison
    8 mistook my client for someone/body
    9 will arrive tomorrow, won't
    10 is a rumour

5   1 falling over/down
    2 fell off
    3 falling about
    4 fall in
    5 fell out
    6 fall off
    7 fell off
    8 fallen through

unit 19 EXPLORATION, ADVENTURE, INVENTION

1   1 C
    2 F
    3 A
    4 E
    5 B

2   1 mountaineers
    2 frightening
    3 defenceless
    4 natural
    5 protection
    6 failure
    7 careful
    8 held
    9 knowledge
    10 indication

3   1 A
    2 B
    3 C
    4 A
    5 D
    6 D
    7 B
    8 A
    9 B
    10 C
    11 A
    12 D
    13 C
    14 A
    15 D

4   1 look at/have/take a look at
    2 wish I could afford
    3 a move on
    4 avoid getting/being stuck in
    5 (even) consider applying
    6 meaning of
    7 as if it will snow/there will be snow
    8 up to Emma to
    9 so tired I can't
    10 had hardly any

5   1 blame
    2 fault
    3 faults
    4 mistake
    5 blamed
    6 fault
    7 mistakes
    8 fault
    9 blame
    10 blamed

unit 20 CONTRASTS

1   1 C
    2 D
    3 D
    4 C
    5 B
    6 B
    7 D
    8 D

2   1 over
    2 until
    3 on
    4 in
    5 at
    6 until/before
    7 until
    8 before
    9 while
    10 as

3   1 being delayed
    2 driving
    3 not to tell
    4 to eat
    5 not warning
    6 to buy
    7 revising

4   1 finding
    2 even, and
    3 from
    4 which
    5 off, near
    6 being
    7 what
    8 at
    9 has
    10 rest, remainder
    11 when, while, as
    12 aboard, on
    13 him
    14 sort, kind
    15 own

5   1 length
    2 weight
    3 found
    4 neighbouring
    5 feed
    6 ability
    7 swimmers
    8 dangerous
    9 resemblance
    10 relatives

8

3 Read the text below. Use the word given in capitals at the end of each line to form a word that fits in the space in the same line. There is an example at the beginning (0).

The Power of the Imagination

Through the centuries, (0) ...... inventors ...... have imagined machines that **INVENT**

were beyond the (1) .... capabilities of their time. Some people **TECHNOLOGY**

imagined machines which are beyond the realms of (2) .... Some **POSSIBLE**

of these machines never went (3) .... than the drawing board. **FAR**

Others were built, tested and rapidly (4) .... Some of the **FORGET**

machines that people believed possible may seem (5) .... to us **RIDICULE**

today. For example, Robert Fludd (1547–1637), the (6) .... of **DESIGN**

a 'perpetual motion' watermill, believed that once it was in (7) .... **OPERATE**

it would continue forever without the (8) .... of an outside power **ASSIST**

source. We now know that the (9) .... parts of a machine produce **MOVE**

friction which slows it down unless it is (10) .... by some kind of power. **DRIVE**

unit 11 THINGS THAT GO WRONG

1 You are going to read a magazine article about a business woman. Eight sentences have been removed from the article. Fill each gap (1–8) with the sentence you think fits best from the list A–I. There is one extra sentence which you do not need to use.

A woman for whom everything went wrong

At the age of 29, Vanessa Brownlow had everything – her own property company, two houses – one in London, one in France – a husband and a baby on the way. One year later she and her son were homeless and penniless. What went wrong?

My parents were quite well off and I grew up in a large, detached house in Surrey. I went to a private girls' school and at the weekend I spent most of the time with my pony. My mother left when I was eight years old and I lived with my father. **1** We also had a housekeeper who ran the house for us.

I was never really close to my father. **2** He was determined that I should be successful. And I accepted this, although of course I knew there was plenty of money behind us, and I can see now that I took this for granted.

After school, my father sent me to a finishing school in Switzerland, and that's where I met a lot of people who became my 'friends'. We all had a lot of money to spend and the assurance that goes with it. **3** In some ways it was, but the most useful asset I had was my ability to get on with people and make the right social contacts. The property business was booming, and I had financial backing from my father that enabled me to get my own company set up. I had a big income, a company Mercedes and a wild social life. When your life's like this, you have no idea about hardship. **4** And you despise people who haven't got any. Looking back, I can see how stupid I was.

Anyway, one night I was out with some friends and I met Max. **5** He was so charming, and seemed so full of original ideas. I wanted to marry him right away, but my father put forward all sorts of objections. I couldn't understand why. Alright, Max didn't have a job, but he had loads of potential and was full of really promising ideas and I was more than willing to guarantee a bank loan to get him started. I put my own houses up as a guarantee. In the end, we got married, but without my father's blessing, and I've never forgiven him for that.

Then I found I was pregnant. I was thrilled about this, but Max wasn't. He didn't seem to like the idea that we'd have to cut down on late nights and going to clubs. And I wasn't well. At one point I had to spend three weeks in hospital. **6** This meant I was going to lose my houses. My business was in deep trouble too. Then my father said he was pulling out his money.

I woke up one morning, eight months pregnant, and Max wasn't there. I had two months in which to leave the house, and my house in France was already on the market. And I just didn't have any cash left. Some friends agreed to pay the bill for the private hospital where the baby was born, and for a few months a friend put us up in her spare room. **7** My father wouldn't help us, and I had to ask the council for somewhere to live. For six months we've been living in this room in accommodation for the homeless. It's horrible – there's thieving all the time, and noise, and I haven't got enough money to keep the room heated. And Daniel, my little boy, gets colds all the time. I feel so hopeless and helpless. None of my 'friends' want to see me, and no one will help. **8** I realise I made too many mistakes – I took money for granted and I was a poor judge of character. I just looked at outward appearances and never looked at what was beneath the surface. I think I brought all this on myself by taking too many things for granted.

A When I came out, I was preoccupied with my health, but I should really have been concentrating on my business affairs. The property market was crashing, and the bank wanted to call in the loan on Max's business.

B We had a succession of au-pairs from France whose job it was to look after me. This was good for my French, which I spoke fluently by the time I left school.

C You haven't got a clue what it's like not to have money.

D But the baby cried a lot at night, and eventually my friend and I fell out and we had to leave.

E I came back to England and did a degree in business studies, as I thought this would be good training for the future.

F I wonder if I will ever get out of this situation, but with no job it's difficult to imagine how things are going to improve.

G Max said he had never wanted to be a father, and he wasn't going to take any responsibility for the baby.

H He was preoccupied with looking after his business affairs, and was happy as long as I produced good school reports.

I I just fell for him.

2

Make a passive construction using the verb in brackets. You will need to use a variety of tenses.

EXAMPLE: John Burton (arrest) if he hadn't fled the country.

ANSWER: John Burton *would have been arrested* if he hadn't fled the country.

1 The books are certainly missing. They (might steal).

2 These works of art have not been seen for decades. They (must destroy) during the war.

3 The acrobats performed a dangerous trick. They (could kill).

4 An antidote to this poison (discover) yet.

5 I bought a copy of *Parade's End* that (sign) by the author in 1930.

6 Max (injure) six times so far in his career as a jockey.

7 Seven candidates (interview) so far.

8 The entire building (clean) every day.

9 The test results (analyse) at this very moment.

10 The college (found) in 1610.

11 Everyone (send) a copy of the agenda before next Monday's meeting.

12 I'm sure the house (sell) eventually.

13 'Those documents (should not give) to the press,' said the minister. 'My secretary made a mistake when he released them.'

14 These scales are supposed (check) every month.

unit **11** THINGS THAT GO WRONG

3 Read the text below and think of the word which best fits each space. Use only one word in each space. There is an example at the beginning (0).

Trapped

Two geology students have been found alive after (0) ..being.. trapped in an old mine for fifteen days. They had (1) .... food at all but survived by drinking rainwater that fell into the mine. They were named today (2) .... John Adams, 20, and Martin Frobisher, 19, both students at Melchester University.

Although very weak, the students were (3) .... to tell their story to reporters. John was leading the way up the slope of a hill. Martin looked back to see how (4) .... they had come. When he turned round again, John was absolutely (5) .... to be seen. He (6) .... vanished. Martin took a few paces forward and found (7) .... falling through space, landing heavily on top of John. Miraculously, (8) .... of the two was injured, despite falling ten metres down an old mine shaft. It was impossible for them to climb out because the sides of the shaft were steep and slippery. They shouted but nobody (9) .... hear their shouts and after a few days they were (10) .... weak to cry out any more.

By (11) .... a shepherd found John's hat, (12) .... had come off when he fell, near the entrance to the shaft. He also saw footprints, guessed (13) .... had happened and called a rescue team. Both students (14) .... definitely have to spend at least a fortnight in hospital to recover (15) .... their ordeal.

unit 11 THINGS THAT GO WRONG

4 Complete the second sentence so that it has a similar meaning to the first sentence. Use the word given and other words to complete each sentence. You must use between two and five words. Do not change the word given.

1 Scientists observed the unusual way the animal behaved.
   was
   The .... observed by scientists.

2 I was more frightened by that film than by any other.
   most
   It was .... film I have ever seen.

3 What are you going to do in the future?
   for
   What are .... future?

4 Nobody has complained about the service before.
   any
   There .... about the service before.

5 Can you explain what went wrong?
   for
   Do you have .... what went wrong?

6 Maria had not spoken to such a large audience before.
   made
   It was the first time Maria .... to such a large audience.

7 There's nothing I wouldn't do to get a ticket to that concert.
   would
   I .... to get a ticket to that concert.

8 Elizabeth has decided not to go to the party after all.
   mind
   Elizabeth has .... to the party.

9 Guy will never forget the first time he visited the zoo.
   always
   Guy will .... to the zoo.

10 The explorers found it difficult to understand what the guide was saying.
   had
   The explorers .... what the guide was saying.

5 Complete the sentences with a phrasal verb based on *pull*.

EXAMPLE: She *pulled back* the curtains and saw it was another lovely day.

1 The child put his hand into the box and .... his favourite toy.

2 The gardener picked up the plant and began to .... the brown leaves.

3 John .... the garage forecourt and stopped in front of the petrol pumps.

4 The bus driver .... into the traffic without even looking at the passing vehicles.

5 Three swimmers were level after three lengths of the pool, but then Anderson .... of the rest.

6 The building was badly damaged in the explosion and had to be ....

7 James had trained hard for the competition but a muscle injury meant he had to .... before the start.

8 The police asked the car driver to .... to the side of the road so they could speak to him.

9 Although the baby was seriously ill, the doctors were confident she would ....

10 He was bitten when he tried to .... the two fighting dogs.

unit 12
WEATHER AND CLIMATE

1 You are going to read a magazine article about weather forecasting. For questions 1–10, choose the answer (A, B, C or D) which you think fits best according to the text.

Come rain or shine

IN THE AMERICAN FILM *Groundhog Day*, Bill Murray plays a television weatherman trapped in time and forced to relive the same day every day. He is cursed to remake an increasingly irritating TV broadcast for ever. When the BBC World Service Television weather presenters relay yet another report of sun and high temperatures for the desert lands of the Middle East, do they get that groundhog feeling?

John Teather, Senior Producer and Head of the BBC Weather Centre, thinks not. 'Part of the technique of weather broadcasting is that you don't dwell on the boring bits. So if there are stable conditions over Arabia you quickly say that and talk instead about the typhoon that is just about to strike Japan. You have to editorialise. The techniques and production values are just the same as any other programme – you have to be interesting and informative. The only difference is we have to do it in a short space of time.'

The nine BBC weathermen and women who make up the team relay their broadcasts from a purpose-built studio at BBC Television Centre in west London. Working in shifts of four people they provide 24-hour coverage: 47 radio and TV broadcasts each weekday and 56 at the weekend.

'To start off we had to learn a lot of geography,' recalls Teather. 'And you have to be sensitive to what people want to hear, to reflect the local agenda. It would be pointless having a presenter in a dark suit telling Hong Kong it is going to be another lovely sunny day when the locals are longing for it to rain because it is too hot.'

It is a high-tech business requiring an impressive range of skills. The weather forecasters – in light-coloured suits on a grey London day – work at full steam throughout each shift. The two weathermen on duty, Peter Cockcroft and Rob McElwee, move from computer screen to Meteorological Office print-out to studio and back.

The BBC bases its forecasts on the information provided by the super computer at the Met Office in Bracknell, Berkshire, which sucks in data every hour from sources around the world. The computer then simulates the world's atmosphere statistically, from sea level, to 30,500 metres, and predicts what is going to happen over the next seven days.

All the forecasters are fully-trained meteorologists and scientists, coming mainly from the Met Office. Teather has the job of picking potential weather forecasters from the staff of civil servants who work there. He tries to define the qualities he looks for.

'It is a magical, unquantifiable ability to communicate. It can't be trained. The meteorologists have an operational science background, so mastering the technology is not a difficulty. The problem is that scientists are trained to be introverts. If you put somebody on who viewers are either going to criticise or be bored with, they don't listen to the message. I get letters from people who say they didn't understand the broadcast. It is not that they didn't understand it, it's that they weren't listening because they didn't like the presenter.'

But can the weather ever be predicted accurately? Edward Lorenz, an American scientist working in the 1960s, suggested that what he termed the 'Butterfly Effect' made long-term weather forecasting inherently imprecise. His research indicated that too many tiny, unpredictable factors – such as local variations in wind speed – would build up over time and destroy accuracy. He suggested that a small difference in the initial state of a weather system can make a significant difference later on.

So if long-term prediction is out, what is left? Teather maintains that the vast international network of statistics and technology means the predictions are generally good. But the general public maintains a level of scepticism about the reliability of any weather forecast. In Britain, apart from the fact that the temperate weather system that operates over the country is difficult to predict, people still remember the violent storms of October 1987 which the forecaster on duty failed to foresee. In other countries some commercial channels have turned the whole thing around by presenting the weather as a kind of comedy routine, as if they no longer expect the public to take their forecasts seriously. Grown weathermen have dressed up as bananas and sung their forecasts.

unit 12 WEATHER AND CLIMATE

1. In the opinion of John Teather, weather forecasters
   - A are sure to get bored with their work.
   - B need to decide what will interest the public.
   - C must select which parts of the world to mention.
   - D should think only of the information they are providing.

2. At the BBC weather centre, weather forecasters
   - A work a 24-hour shift.
   - B have a free choice about what to wear for work.
   - C are short of time to relax when they are working.
   - D must be good at teamwork.

3. BBC weather forecasts are
   - A dependent on the analysis made by forecasters themselves.
   - B able to use information from around the world.
   - C forced to concentrate on information regarding Britain.
   - D give information in the form of statistics.

4. People being considered for jobs as weather forecasters
   - A already have media experience.
   - B are trained scientists.
   - C need psychological training.
   - D are selected for their computer skills.

5. In the opinion of Lorenz,
   - A short-term forecasting is inaccurate.
   - B forecasters consider too many factors when making reports.
   - C the state of the weather is influenced by tiny events.
   - D local conditions make general predictions unsound.

6. The general public thinks forecasters
   - A are better than nothing.
   - B are rarely reliable.
   - C are not worth paying attention to.
   - D should disappear from TV.

2 Choose the correct phrase for the gap in each sentence.

> by the time   so   because   because of
> even though   as if   just as   so that
> as long as   but   in case   whose
> in which   despite   so as not to

1. Jack ran 40 kilometres .... couldn't finish the marathon.
2. Mary picked up the baby carefully .... wake it up.
3. James placed the camera inside his shirt .... it couldn't be seen.
4. .... I got to the cinema, the film was almost over.
5. Tom looks .... he has spent half an hour on the rowing machine.
6. I don't get paid until Friday, ... I can't pay you back until then.
7. .... I arrived very early, there was already a long queue.
8. .... I got to the front of the queue, the ticket office closed.
9. Martin wore sandals .... the freezing weather.
10. This is the cave .... the treasure was found.
11. You can borrow the sports equipment .... you clean it after use.
12. .... his illness, Bernard could not attend the meeting.
13. Is that the lady .... picture was in the newspaper last week?
14. Take some sandwiches with you .... you feel hungry later on.
15. The children can't see that film .... they are not old enough.

51

unit **12** WEATHER AND CLIMATE

3 Read the text below and decide which answer (A, B, C, or D) best fits each space. Put a circle round the letter that you choose. The exercise begins with an example (0).

Light Pollution

We all know that pollution can be (0) .... by too much rubbish, too many chemicals and too much noise. An excessive (1) .... of artificial light may also be considered a (2) .... of pollution. Towns and cities, especially in the northern hemisphere (3) .... such an enormous quantity of light that many of the stars that should be visible to the (4) .... eye cannot be seen at all. In many countries, you have to go (5) .... out into the countryside to see a night sky that is worth looking at. Even there, the glow from (6) .... cities may (7) .... into a significant proportion of the sky. Many observatories in remote places have had to (8) .... because astronomers can no longer get a good (9) .... of the sky. Many children have never seen the star-filled night skies that their grandparents were (10) .... with.

Street lights, the main cause of the (11) ...., are often so badly-designed that half their light goes into the sky instead of onto the road. Many people (12) .... brightly-lit streets on the grounds that criminals are (13) ...., but the bright lights also leave areas of deep, black (14) .... where nothing can be seen, especially by eyes which have got accustomed to (15) .... light.

0	A	caused	B	made	C	enlarged	D	originated
1	A	creation	B	lot	C	amount	D	measure
2	A	form	B	way	C	result	D	factor
3	A	give	B	have	C	produce	D	project
4	A	naked	B	open	C	clear	D	sharp
5	A	deep	B	far	C	long	D	up
6	A	busy	B	industrialised	C	horizontal	D	distant
7	A	lighten	B	reflect	C	go	D	extend
8	A	close	B	stop	C	end	D	cease
9	A	observation	B	view	C	regard	D	panorama
10	A	familiar	B	granted	C	brought	D	experienced
11	A	difficulty	B	disaster	C	situation	D	problem
12	A	enjoy	B	maintain	C	defend	D	argue
13	A	avoided	B	deterred	C	prevented	D	stopped
14	A	shadow	B	dark	C	blankness	D	shade
15	A	full	B	extreme	C	shining	D	strong

4 For questions 1–15, read the text and look carefully at each line. Some of the lines are correct and some have a word which should not be there. Write the wrong word in the space provided and tick the correct lines. There are two examples at the beginning (0) and (00).

SOAKED TO THE SKIN

Our recent camping trip to Scotland was, I am sorry to say, a	0 ✓
complete disaster because it had rained non-stop on every day	00 had
of our four-day 'adventure'. It is true that during the first hour	1 ....
of our walk, the sun was shining on and it was dry, but all of a	2 ....
sudden the sky darkened, the storm clouds gathered themselves	3 ....
and the rain fell out. Of course, we put waterproof jackets on but	4 ....
by the evening our boots and socks were wet through. After we	5 ....
had put our tents up, in the rain, we tried to light a fire to do cook	6 ....
on but it was an impossible, so we had to eat cold food from tins.	7 ....
In the morning, we had to put our wet boots back on, although we	8 ....
had such dry socks but after walking for a short time they were wet	9 ....
too. By the end of the second day, the rain had penetrated at our	10 ....
rucksacks and made our sleepings bags and spare clothes most wet.	11 ....
On the third day our jackets could no longer keep out of the rain and	12 ....
our trousers were caked with mud up to the knees. We felt as we	13 ....
were walking on the bottom of the sea and we dreamed of some long	14 ....
hot baths. Our ordeal lasted another day before we reached to our	15 ....
destination.	

53

unit 13 HEROES AND HEROINES?

1 You are going to read a magazine article about the Wild West. For questions 1–14 choose from the people (A–E). Some of the people may be used more than once. When more than one answer is required, these may be given in any order. For questions 15 and 16, choose the answer A, B, C or D that you think fits best.

Who

was killed by a colleague?	1	
had a job upholding the law?	2	3 ....
fought as a soldier?	4	5 ....
lost parents when young?	6	
was shot by a lawman?	7	
enjoyed gambling?	8	
is famous for killing several members of the same family?	9	
died an old man?	10	
is said to have killed as many men as he had years?	11	
planned robberies?	12	13 ....
is said to have killed ten times more men than he actually did?	14	

A BILLY THE KID
B FRANK JAMES
C JESSE JAMES
D WILD BILL HICKOK
E WYATT EARP

15 In the Wild West, the number of men killed by gunmen
   A is greater than generally thought.
   B was underestimated by the killers.
   C was exaggerated by lawmen.
   D is difficult to establish.

16 It is a fact about the Wild West that
   A citizens enjoyed observing gunfights.
   B men did not usually carry guns.
   C guns were not reliable.
   D gunfights occurred frequently.

54

The Law of the Gun

Two men – one good, one bad – stand facing each other, less than 100 feet apart, on the deserted main street of a frontier town. Nervous citizens peer through saloon windows and around the corners of buildings. As the two men slowly step towards each other, their hands hover above the handles of six-shooters in holsters at their hips. In less than the blink of an eye, weapons are drawn. Gunshots shatter the stillness. One man lies dead or dying, his blood staining the dust.

A typical Western gunfight? Only as imagined time and again by Hollywood or in countless novels. The reality of the West's law of the gun was very different. One thing was true, however: the West could be a lawless place. The second half of the nineteenth century was a turbulent time, with the Mexico–USA War of 1846–47 followed by the Gold Rush of '49 and, a decade later, the Civil War. A generation of Western men came of age with guns in their hands. Though most carried them merely for hunting, for defence against wild animals, or just for macho swagger, a significant number of men nonetheless believed that a bullet could speak louder and more decisively than any written law – especially in a land where the social order was barely a few years old.

It was frequently hard to tell on which side of justice people stood. Take the legendary Wild Bill Hickok. He secured his reputation as a gunfighter by killing a rival card player and later, when he was marshal of Abilene, Kansas, he directed operations from a poker table in one of the town's grandest saloons. Bank robbers Frank and Jesse James were cheered by farming folk, who saw their thievery and killing as acts of revenge on the Union victors of the Civil War.

But, in fact, shoot-outs seldom occurred, and gunfighter's boasts of the number of men they killed were usually vastly inflated. The outlaw Billy the Kid, according to legend, killed 21 men, one for each year he lived; but close study of the historical records shows a more likely death toll of six. Wild Bill Hickok supposedly dispatched over 100 bad men; ten was closer to the truth.

The image of two men with guns pacing out the distance between them as they followed some unwritten code is another myth. In the real West, most gunfighters – or, as they were more likely to call themselves then, man-killers or shootists – shot it out wherever, whenever and however they could. For many years, handguns were dangerously untrustworthy – inaccurate and quite likely to misfire or even explode in the hand. Given the revolver's questionable accuracy, being quick on the draw was no guarantee of advantage. Some gunfighters, in fact, gained fame – and, more importantly, stayed alive – thanks to their cool bearing under pressure.

The good, the bad or the unlucky?

Billy the Kid: Orphaned at age fourteen in Sante Fe, New Mexico, William H. Bonney drifted into petty thievery. The flamboyant, intelligent, polite misfit committed his first murder before his eighteenth birthday. The 1878 Lincoln Country Land Wars provided an outlet for his taste for blood. Sheriff Pat Garrett gunned Billy down two months before he was 22.

Frank and Jesse James: After the Civil War, the James brothers returned to their native Missouri and formed the James Gang, applying their military skills to robbing banks and trains. Gang member Robert Ford murdered Jesse for a $10,000 reward in 1882. Frank retired, dying in 1915.

Wild Bill Hickok: James Butler Hickok's exploits as gunfighter, lawman and gambler earned him the nickname Wild Bill. During a poker game in Deadwood, South Dakota, in 1876, Hickok was shot dead while holding two black eights, two black aces and a jack of diamonds – forever after known as 'dead man's hand'.

Wyatt Earp: Born in Illinois, Earp served as an assistant marshal in Dodge City, Kansas, in the 1870s. He and two brothers, Virgil and Morgan, were reportedly involved in robbery and murder. Their shoot-out at the OK Corral in October, 1881, silenced the Clanton family, who may have had evidence against them.

unit **13** HEROES AND HEROINES?

2 Read the text below and think of the word which best fits each space. Use only one word in each space. There is an example at the beginning (0).

The interesting life of Alan Bean

Alan Bean (0) ......was...... born in 1932 in Texas, USA. He developed (1) .... early interest in aviation and spent a lot of time making model aeroplanes. At the age of eighteen, he won a US Navy scholarship (2) .... enabled him to study aeronautical engineering at the University of Texas. When he graduated, he learned to fly and spent five years (3) .... a Navy pilot. Later he became a test pilot and (4) .... was at this time that he had a lucky escape. An aircraft he was flying (5) .... struck by lightning but he managed to land it safely, (6) .... it was badly damaged.

In 1962, he applied for the NASA astronaut training programme and a year (7) .... was selected as one of the fourteen astronauts who (8) .... take part in the Apollo missions to the Moon. In 1969, he became the fourth man to (9) .... foot on the surface of the Moon, (10) .... he spent 31 hours, collecting rock samples and carrying (11) .... scientific experiments. He went into space a second time in 1973 (12) .... he was commander of Skylab. He and his crew spent 59 days in space, a record (13) .... that time.

After spending a (14) .... of years training astronauts, Alan Bean retired and devoted more time to his favourite hobby. He is a keen painter, (15) .... of pictures of his experiences in space.

unit 13 HEROES AND HEROINES?

3 Complete the second sentence so that it has a similar meaning to the first sentence. Use the word given and other words to complete each sentence. You must use between two and five words. Do not change the word given.

1 Roderick was frightened of the unknown, so he didn't open the cellar door.
from
Roderick's fear of the unknown .... the cellar door.

2 Jane was ill for three weeks.
get
Jane took three weeks .... her illness.

3 You will not find it difficult to translate this letter.
no
You will .... this letter.

4 Bernard is one of my friends from college.
mine
Bernard .... from college.

5 To our surprise, the weather changed suddenly.
by
We were .... in the weather.

6 Every film he appeared in made the actor more and more popular.
with
The actor's .... every film he appeared in.

7 Despite his appearance, Mr Taylor is not in good health.
as
Mr Taylor .... he looks.

8 The motor-cyclist was so seriously injured he could not be moved.
were
The motor-cyclist's .... that he could not be moved.

9 I could tell she was reluctant to help me from the tone of her voice.
revealed
Her tone of voice .... to help me.

10 Sarah recovered from her illness very quickly.
swift
Sarah .... from her illness.

4 Complete the sentences with a phrasal verb based on *push*.

EXAMPLE: John's a tough little boy and won't allow himself to be *pushed around* .

1 There was a strong feeling that the new law should quickly be .... Parliament.

2 Fans rushed up to the singer but the police .... them ....

3 There was a long queue for the bus and the visitor tried to .... his way ....

4 There was a fight and the man tried to .... the woman .... the cliff.

5 The shortage of raw material .... the cost of the manufactured goods.

6 When everyone was in the boat, Charles picked up the oar and .... from the river bank.

7 Although the weather was getting worse, the climbers decided to .... towards the summit.

8 In the rush to get to the exit, the crowd .... the barriers blocking their way.

unit 14 VICTIMS AND VILLAINS

1 You are going to read a newspaper article about a young offender. Six paragraphs have been removed from the article. Fill each gap (1–6) with the paragraph which you think fits best from the list A–G. There is one extra paragraph which you do not need to use.

A date with the burglar

My daughter's radio was on the front step; the kitchen window frame had been smashed. Upstairs, the wardrobe was open, its contents spread out on the bed. All the drawers were tipped out on the floor. We had been burgled. Again.

1

It seemed a young age to start on a life of petty crime. I don't believe that, as a journalist, I am particularly naive, but I didn't want one so young to go to prison for any material things we had owned. I think people are infinitely more important.

2

The magistrate said that he had never seen a letter like it. He decided to postpone the sentence Paul would suffer for six months.

3

I gave this a lot of thought and told Paul I would stay with him and see what we could do. I told him I wanted nothing from him, that he was forgiven and that I hoped to be able to offer him an opportunity to make his own decisions.

4

Eventually Paul had to go back to the court for sentencing on both burglaries, mine and the larger one. He met me at our local station looking smart. I had bought him a blue blazer for his eighteenth birthday and given him a tie. I told him I wanted him to look more like a lawyer than a criminal.

5

A year later, a solicitor phoned me at my office and said Paul had been arrested on cheque card charges and had given my name as his next of kin. He wanted legal aid. I undertook to get it and to visit him that weekend. He was nervous, ill at ease, when we met. I said we had to get our priorities right, that we were in trouble and had to see what best we could do. I wrote to the court, and appeared with him. Paul was given two years, of which he served just over a year. I wrote to him and visited him often.

6

Well, should victims meet their attackers? I don't know. I know only that I am grateful for what has happened in this case. I am proud of Paul and the effort he has made.

58

unit **14** VICTIMS AND VILLAINS

A It was only then that I learned that Paul owed a £100 fine for handling stolen goods. There was an assault charge against him, and worse, there were charges over a burglary involving goods worth upwards of £15,000 which had been taken by him and others unnamed.

B The judge was very helpful. He gave Paul a two-year conditional discharge on both crimes and advised him to stay close to me and his future would look bright.

C There was a perfect handprint on a window. Paul was arrested nine months later. I read of the case in our local paper. He had already spent three months at a 'short, sharp shock centre'. A custodial sentence was in view. He was seventeen.

D I have met his mother, his real father, his brother and sisters. I have spent part of each subsequent Christmas with them. The first Christmas Paul sent us a large box of chocolates and a card.

E Paul has now been out of prison for five years, and has done no wrong. I believe he has made his decisions. Paul has a small flat. I see him now and then. If he needs help or advice, he phones me.

F I saw Paul through eighteen days in Chelmsford prison over the assault charge and lodged an appeal since I was convinced he was innocent and I wanted it off his record. But we dropped the appeal because publicity would have cost him the job I helped him to get.

G All I proposed trying to do was to keep him out of prison. I phoned the probation service and reached Paul's probation officer. He expressed some surprise, but told me to write him a letter which he would place before the clerk of the court.

---

2 Complete the sentences with the correct preposition.

EXAMPLE: Julia congratulated me ...*on*... winning the prize.

1 Don't rely .... Jack. He'll let you down.

2 The unit price depends .... how many you buy.

3 For the next four weeks, I have to concentrate .... revising for the exam.

4 You need to see a doctor who specialises .... this area of medicine.

5 Bernard suffers .... severe headaches.

6 On his third attempt, the champion succeeded .... lifting the weight.

7 Many people objected .... the new work schedule.

8 Who paid .... the meal?

9 Martin believes .... taking out lots of life insurance.

10 The accountant insisted .... being shown all the receipts.

3 Complete the sentences, using either *borrow* or *lend*, as appropriate. Remember to put the verb in the correct form.

EXAMPLE: Could I possibly ...*borrow*... your pen?

1 Many students have to .... money to finance their studies.

2 Money .... are rarely popular people.

3 John worked overtime to make enough money to pay back what he had ....

4 I had to ask my sister to .... me a dress for the party.

5 More than a thousand people .... books from the library each week.

6 Do you know anyone who could .... you a backpack for the trip?

7 Martin had .... the suit from his father, but it was far too big for him.

8 Last week I .... my camera to Alice and she dropped it.

9 Helen repaid the £500 she .... from the bank within three months.

10 .... money is never cheap.

unit **14** VICTIMS AND VILLAINS

4 Read the text below and decide which answer (A, B, C or D) best fits each space. Put a circle round the letter that you choose. The exercise begins with an example (0).

SIX CONVICTED KILLERS DIG OUT OF FLORIDA PRISON

Helicopters (**0**) .... sugar cane fields from the air as 100 officers (**1**) .... tracker dogs across south-central Florida, hoping to lock onto the (**2**) .... of five escaped murderers. John Townsend, prison superintendent, speculated that the men may be (**3**) .... advantage of the watery landscape to hide from their pursuers. The (**4**) ...., wet soil certainly made it easy to dig the tunnel that (**5**) .... them below the prison's razor-wire fence. He said the escapees could be hiding in sugar cane fields or irrigation ditches, (**6**) .... hollow canes as snorkels to breathe with.

The breakout was (**7**) .... when the escapees (**8**) .... alarms as they made their (**9**) .... under the fence. Guards fired several shots as they popped up from their 20-metre tunnel and (**10**) .... One prisoner was recaptured right away.

The prisoners dug the tunnel below the prison chapel. While other prisoners prayed and sang, one of the six would slip below the floor, which was (**11**) .... off the ground. Once (**12**) ...., the digger would change into a spare (**13**) .... of clothes and dig with his hands or spoons. Before leaving, he would change back into his clean uniform. Plans for the tunnel began taking (**14**) .... about two months ago and it (**15**) .... three weeks to dig it, according to the recaptured prisoner.

0	A hunted	B scanned	C covered	**D searched**
1	A led	B walked	C accompanied	D conducted
2	A traces	B tracks	C smells	D footprints
3	A taking	B enjoying	C experiencing	D getting
4	A fresh	B soft	C smooth	D creamy
5	A escaped	B ran	C carried	D took
6	A using	B making	C having	D keeping
7	A remarked	B found	C discovered	D realised
8	A set off	B set up	C set by	D set out
9	A way	B path	C approach	D route
10	A ran over	B ran off	C ran down	D ran through
11	A mounted	B escalated	C raised	D heightened
12	A placed	B through	C done	D there
13	A pile	B collection	C pair	D set
14	A form	B direction	C shape	D control
15	A was	B took	C worked	D spent

5 Complete the second sentence so that it has a similar meaning to the first sentence. Use the word given and other words to complete each sentence. You must use between two and five words. Do not change the word given.

1. 'We must conclude that he lied to us,' said the Inspector.
   lie
   'Obviously, he ....,' said the Inspector.

2. The headmaster said how very disappointed he was with the exam results.
   great
   The headmaster expressed .... with the exam results.

3. The Sunrise Travel Agency arranged my journey for me.
   were
   The .... made by the Sunrise Travel Agency.

4. I was astonished when Sybille made up her mind to leave the company.
   at
   I was astonished .... to leave the company.

5. It is not necessary to get to the station early.
   no
   There .... to get to the station early.

6. The spectators got more and more excited as the match continued.
   of
   The .... as the match continued.

7. Anna was completely uninterested in the television documentary.
   showed
   Anna .... in the television documentary.

8. The runaway elephant greatly alarmed the villagers.
   great
   The runaway elephant .... in the village.

9. The way their son behaves is a source of worry to Mr and Mrs Smith.
   about
   Mr and Mrs Smith .... behaviour.

10. The information the tourist office gave us was not correct.
    by
    We .... the tourist office.

6 Complete the sentences with a phrasal verb based on *turn*.

EXAMPLE: When the summer came we didn't need the central heating so we *turned* it *off*.

1. I had to .... the sound on the TV in order to hear what the caller was saying on the telephone.

2. I wonder how many people will .... for the meeting?

3. Stephen's request for a day off was ....

4. We thought it was going to rain today but it has .... to be quite sunny.

5. In the accident with the lorry the car was pushed over the bank and .... onto its roof.

6. It's past my bedtime – I'd better ....

7. I didn't like Anna as a child but she has .... to be a pleasant young woman.

8. Bad weather forced the climbers to .... , abandoning their climb.

9. I heard a voice behind me and .... to see who it was.

10. Before leaving the studio, Alex checked he had .... all the electrical equipment.

unit 15 LIES, TRICKS AND DECEIT

1 You are going to read a magazine article about a trip in Canada. Six paragraphs have been removed from the article. Fill each gap (1–6) with the paragraph you think fits best from the list A–G. There is one extra paragraph which you do not need to use.

Riding the rocky road to ruin

We thought we had a winner when after advertising for a lift around the Canadian Rockies, Christian turned up and offered to drive me and Martene wherever we wanted. It was too good to be true.

1

The next morning, Christian and another guy found that their wallets had been stolen. Christian assured us that he would be able to have some money sent to him so we might as well continue our journey, but he asked if we could lend him some money. I did.

We set off for Jasper and when we stopped for lunch, Martene discovered her travellers' cheques were gone.

2

Once in Jasper, Martene was finally able to ring and cancel her credit card. She also rang about her travellers' cheques and was told she could pick up some in the morning. This meant going back to Banff, and we set off the next morning.

3

Not once did we think Christian had stolen Martene's money or credit card. Why should we? Occasionally, Martene had left her money bag in the car, but only for about five minutes. Besides, Christian was so helpful and sympathetic. But Martene and I did think it odd that he always paid for everything when we weren't around and he never once asked us for money for petrol.

4

A week after setting out with Christian, we found ourselves staying in a hostel not far from Jasper. It was snowing so Martene and I decided to take only our backpacks out of the car and get the rest of our things later. We had just paid for our accommodation when the manager came and asked us about Christian's car – did we know what sort of car it was, and did we know the number plate? Martene and I didn't know.

5

At first we couldn't believe it but once we started thinking back to all the things that had happened, it started to make sense.

6

We both realised how stupid we had been: we'd set out with a stranger without getting any details at all. We were fortunate that it was only our coats, some money and a few items that he had stolen. It could have been worse. He could have done us harm. Unfortunately, Martene later learnt that Christian had spent 800 dollars on her credit card. We both learnt our lesson.

A We wondered what was going on. Fortunately, I still had some money, and Christian told us not to worry, as he'd soon have some money and he had some friends who lived not far from Jasper who would put us up for free.

B We also noticed that Christian never said much about his personal life and refused to stay at the larger hostels.

C On the second day, we had our first unlucky break. We were staying in a hostel just outside the town of Banff when Martene discovered that her credit card was missing. Fortunately, we still had her travellers' cheques. She would have to cancel the card later as the nearest telephone was an hour away.

D Martene and I rang the police and reported what had happened but there wasn't much they could do as we didn't have many details. We didn't even know Christian's surname.

E We found Banff to be a delightful town and we were glad to have the chance to stay in a private house there, instead of in the usual hostel.

F We didn't think any more about it but then the manager came back and told us that Christian had gone. He had been trying to pay for his accommodation with a stolen credit card. It was Christian all along who was doing the stealing.

G After Martene had collected her travellers' cheques, Christian picked up his cash card and tried to withdraw some cash. The card didn't work. It looked like it was going to be some time before I got back the money he owed me.

Satellites

Since the late (0) __fifties__, thousands of artificial satellites have been   FIFTY

put in the Earth's orbit. Many are now out of (1) _____, just scrap metal   ACT

in space, which may be involved in (2) _____ with useful satellites.   COLLIDE

Some satellites provide (3) _____ information for weather forecasting.   RELY

Others can measure (4) _____ in the earth's crust which may indicate   MOVE

earthquake (5) _____ in the near future. There are satellites which can   ACTIVE

indicate the exact (6) _____ of forest fires long before they could be   LOCATE

spotted by (7) _____ on Earth. Some satellites have sensitive   OBSERVE

photographic (8) _____ which can show how well crops are growing   EQUIP

in the fields and make (9) _____ of rivers and deserts. In the future,   MEASURE

satellites, in the form of giant mirrors, could provide (10) _____   ILLUMINATE

for cities and roads by reflecting the sun's rays onto Earth's nightside.

unit **15** LIES, TRICKS AND DECEIT

3 Read the text below and look carefully at each line. Some of the lines are correct and some have a word which should not be there. Write the wrong word in the space provided and tick the correct lines. There are two examples at the beginning (0) and (00).

Cheated

Maria and I were recently been cheated out of quite a large sum	0	been
of money. We wanted to go to a concert but we were told that	00	✓
every ticket had already been sold out. When we left the ticket	1	
office we met us a man in the street who offered to sell two tickets	2	
that he no longer had needed. He wanted £40 each instead of	3	
being £20 each, which is the official price, but we agreed to buy	4	
them because of we really wanted to go to the concert. We gave	5	
him two £50 notes and he gave us a £20 note as change. When we	6	
went to the concert, last Saturday, we were not allowed to enter in.	7	
The officials told us that our tickets were forgeries, not as genuine	8	
tickets at all. We were very disappointed and to make the matters	9	
worse, we also discovered that the £20 note was a forgery. A	10	
shop assistant looked at it so closely and would not accept it. There	11	
is nothing much what we can do about it. We reported everything	12	
to the police but they will probably not be able to find the man who	13	
tricked us out of our money. We must learn from an experience and	14	
be a lot more careful about buying tickets for concerts in future times.	15	

64

unit 15 LIES, TRICKS AND DECEIT

4 Here are some common mistakes made by students at First Certificate level. Write out these sentences correctly.

1 Martin enjoyed very much to look after his pet snake.
   ....

2 The news were far worse than I expected.
   ....

3 Don't have a sunbath for more than thirty minutes.
   ....

4 You will have to work hardly until you will finish.
   ....

5 After the storm, we could see that the damages were not serious.
   ....

6 My new office is nearby my house so I want spend a lot of money on the travel to work.
   ....

7 I have always liked the nature.
   ....

8 John has succeeded to get a better job.
   ....

9 As my father, I love play golf.
   ....

10 Sally is quiet an intelligent child.
   ....

11 Now a days, most of people have a car.
   ....

12 Jack speaks fluently the Greek.
   ....

13 I like visit the art galleries.
   ....

14 Sarah flies to United States tomorrow.
   ....

15 In this part of the country, it uses to be very cold most of the year.
   ....

16 My favourite subject is economy.
   ....

17 They arrived to Edinburgh since three weeks.
   ....

18 My grandfather would not accept to show me the letters.
   ....

19 Tom adviced me don't visit the exhibition.
   ....

20 I will buy the book as soon as I will go into town.
   ....

unit 16
A THING OF BEAUTY IS A JOY FOREVER

1 You are going to read a newspaper article about an artist. Seven sentences have been removed from the article. Fill each gap (1–7) with the sentence which you think fits best from the list A–H. There is one sentence which you do not need to use.

Painter who lost his sight 'sees' as sculptor

In 1926, when Franco Marzotto Caotorta was twelve, he underwent an eye operation which involved cutting into the retina to correct severe short-sightedness. But at the age of 54, after a gradual deterioration in his eyesight, he went blind. **1** ☐ He was, he said, one of 500 people who were to lose their eyesight within decades of having that operation.

But like artists from Michelangelo to Monet, who carried on working even when their eyes let them down, Mr Caotorta did not give up creating. **2** ☐ Working initially in clay, and then plasteline, a material that is particularly easy to mould, he trained himself, inspired by remembered images of Renaissance sculpture. **3** ☐ And still, he said, 'It takes me a long time. I have a model, just there for the proportions, to tell me how long is an arm, an elbow…' Striving for realism, he feels his model's features, '**4** ☐ Otherwise it doesn't exist.'

Finally, at the age of 80, Mr Caotorta is preparing to make his British debut, with three exhibitions, including such distinguished venues as Hatfield House in Hertfordshire and the Accademia Italiana in central London. His achievements are remarkable. **5** ☐ Degas, for example, lost the use of his right eye and may have suffered from severely weakened eyesight as early as his thirties: he often wrote of his anguish over his sight. **6** ☐ And by 1537, when he had reached the age of 62, Michelangelo could no longer carry out detailed work at close range.

A number of historians have suggested that extreme short-sightedness was not only reflected in some artists' work, but may have affected it. It has been said that colour changes in Monet's late water lily paintings were due to his failing eyesight, a result of cataracts. **7** ☐

Mr Caortorta said that he was spurred on not by the example of any artist, but by a 'necessity'. When he went blind, he was not 'desperate or sad… I was so helped by my family. It came so naturally to be blind.'

A And I visualise the image in my mind.

B He became a sculptor and his hands became his eyes, his memory and touch his guides.

C Mr Caotorta will be exhibiting in the State Rooms of Hatfield House from May and in London at the Quaker Gallery, in St Martin's Lane from 21 June and the Accademia Italiana in Rutland Gate from 6 July.

D In 1918, he wrote of no longer perceiving colours with the same intensity.

E Mr Caotorta, who by then had established himself as a painter of Tuscan landscapes, exhibiting in galleries in Milan and Rome, was forced to lay down his brushes for the last time.

F Yet there are a surprising number of great masters who suffered such severe deterioration of their eyesight that they might have been registered as partially sighted.

G Pissarro was unable to paint out of doors because of his eyes' sensitivity to light and wind.

H At first he was not confident of his abilities and it took some fifteen years before he felt he was skilled enough to have his sculptures cast in bronze.

2 Read the text below. Use the word given in capitals at the end of each line to form a word that fits in the space in the same line. There is an example at the beginning (0).

THE JURASSIC TREE

Scientists in Australia have announced the (0) __discovery__ of a tree　　**DISCOVER**

which was (1) .... to have become extinct in the Jurassic era, 150　　**THINK**

million years ago, when dinosaurs ruled the Earth. The (2) .... of　　**LOCATE**

the trees (there are about 40) is a secret, for (3) .... reasons,　　**SECURE**

but they are in an almost (4) .... part of the Blue Mountains　　**ACCESS**

in south-eastern Australia. Botanists have reacted with (5) ....　　**ASTONISH**

at the news. 'It's like finding a small dinosaur still (6) .... on　　**LIVE**

Earth,' said one. 'It's certainly the most (7) .... botanical find　　**SIGNIFY**

this century. The (8) .... of these trees is almost unbelievable.'　　**SURVIVE**

The trees are about 40 metres in (9) .... and have unusual bark　　**HIGH**

like bubbly brown chocolate. The worldwide (10) .... of these trees　　**POPULAR**

will be guaranteed if scientists can grow them from seed.

unit **16** A THING OF BEAUTY IS A JOY FOREVER

3 Read the text below and decide which answer (A, B, C or D) best fits each space. Put a circle round the letter that you choose. The exercise begins with an example (0).

How old is it?

Many objects found by archaeologists in their (0) .... are very valuable. They may be rare or made of (1) .... metals. They may be works of art or objects that (2) .... vital information about ancient civilisations. Some people forge archaeological artefacts, either to (3) .... money or to become famous. Until the 1950s, when carbon-14 dating came into (4) .... , archaeologists could easily be (5) .... by fakes or (6) .... develop mistaken ideas about the development of ancient civilisations. Carbon-14 dating (7) .... archaeology but it does have some disadvantages. It can only be used for objects of plant or animal (8) .... It is also necessary for a small part of the object to be destroyed when carbon-14 dating takes (9) .... Archaeologists may be unwilling to do this in the (10) .... of a really valuable object.

Archaeologists also (11) .... X-rays to see what is inside objects such as statues. Forgeries tend to have cheaper (12) .... on the inside. There are also various chemical tests for metal, glass and ceramic objects. As the (13) .... of manufacture has changed over the centuries, (14) .... chemicals are present or absent in objects of a particular period. All in all, there are so many accurate dating (15) .... available that a successful archaeological forgery is almost impossible.

0	A digging	(B) excavations	C sites	D underground
1	A invaluable	B priceless	C precious	D expensive
2	A reveal	B contain	C have	D send
3	A possess	B make	C save	D take
4	A play	B fashion	C use	D action
5	A taken in	B taken over	C taken up	D taken out
6	A especially	B only	C rather	D simply
7	A revised	B renewed	C liberated	D revolutionised
8	A type	B origin	C nature	D stuff
9	A place	B part	C issue	D position
10	A example	B case	C view	D manner
11	A develop	B have	C use	D regard
12	A substance	B matter	C material	D things
13	A work	B means	C style	D process
14	A the	B certain	C named	D any
15	A systems	B ways	C experiments	D techniques

4 Complete the second sentence so that it has a similar meaning to the first sentence. Use the word given and other words to complete each sentence. You must use between two and five words. Do not change the word given.

1 Did Mr Brown say anything about the meeting tomorrow?
   mention
   Did Mr Brown .... meeting?

2 John's suggestion was to deliver the parcel personally.
   suggested
   John .... the parcel personally.

3 You must practise tennis for three hours every day.
   of
   Three hours .... every day is essential for you.

4 Martin resented his friend's success more and more.
   at
   Martin's .... his friend's success grew and grew.

5 I'm not completely familiar with this computer.
   used
   I'm not .... this computer.

6 Mary is interested in knowing more about palaeontology.
   like
   Mary .... more about palaeontology.

7 Why did the coach choose new players?
   were
   Why .... the coach?

8 This is an old watch so you need to wind it up.
   needs
   This watch .... because it is an old one.

9 It's possible that Jane didn't get the message.
   a
   There .... that Jane didn't get the message.

10 There is no point in asking Peter.
    pointless
    It's .... Peter.

5 Complete the sentences with the appropriate verb – *say*, *speak*, *talk* or *tell* – in the correct form.

1 What did the inspector .... when you .... him you had lost your ticket?

2 At what age do children learn to .... the time?

3 What do you .... to the idea of eating out tonight?

4 I couldn't find anyone who could .... English.

5 John gets annoyed if people .... while the film is showing.

6 Let's make an early start tomorrow, ... at 5 a.m.?

7 Robert .... jokes better than anyone else I know.

8 After his accident, Tom was unable to .... for several weeks.

9 Miss Bates never stops .... and what she .... is not interesting.

10 Mrs Jones was upset at being .... to so impolitely.

unit 17 A SENSE OF ACHIEVEMENT

1 You are going to read a magazine interview with an American film director. Choose the most suitable heading from the list A–I for each part (1–7) of the article. There is one extra heading which you do not need to use. There is an example at the beginning (0).

A Are you afraid of failure?
B What odd jobs have you had?
C When did you decide to become a film-maker?
D What was the worst career advice you have been given?
E What were the greatest influences on you as a film-maker?
F Your name is Gus Van Sant Junior. Who was Gus Van Sant Senior and what career did he envisage for his son?
G Do you have any hobbies outside the world of film-making?
H Do you ever dream about your films?
I What did you dream about becoming when you were a child?

GUS VAN SANT – FILM DIRECTOR

Director of *Drugstore Cowboy*,
My Own Private Idaho and *Even Cowgirls Get the Blues*.

0 I

I wanted to be a painter and then later, when I was still pretty young, I wanted to be a film-maker. The kind of paintings I made were sort of figurative and I painted landscapes. I also did photography all along so that the visual side all worked together when I started film-making.

1

It happened when I was in art school in the early '70s. I was about 20. I bought a camera and started making films of my own, because painting seemed to be a tough way to go businesswise. As soon as I started to work more on film, that kind of consumed me because it was so difficult, and it's still that way.

2

He was an executive in the fashion business and he envisioned his son to be in the same business too, but I didn't really take to it so it didn't work out that way.

3

I was working on Madison Avenue in advertising in 1969. I also worked as a night janitor, mostly just cleaning and stuff. I could think while I worked but it didn't really present an opportunity to do much more than get on with the job in hand. I also worked in a chemical factory mixing dangerous chemicals and paint when I was 21.

4

My father tried to talk me out of the film business at one point to come work in his company, so I guess that was bad advice because it's worked out quite well for me and it wouldn't have done if I'd listened to him.

5

Yeah, I think about them before they're made when they're just ideas and then during the making of them when it's sort of harnessing of the ideas. But that's what they are before they're made, they're just dreams. They don't disturb my sleep.

6

No, because if I was then I probably wouldn't be doing the things that I am doing just because of the sheer fear of exactly that.

7

I still take a lot of pictures and I paint. I do a regular amount of reading. Some of my films have even come from a novel or something I have read. I'm reading Marshall McLuhan at the moment, who's not really a storyteller but a media theoretician. I don't think there's anything you can make a film of in there, although I just made a film that's about a character who's influenced by her desire to be on television. Notoriety has always been a human obsession, it's just that now the media is our main form of communicating it.

unit 17 A SENSE OF ACHIEVEMENT

2 Complete the sentences with the appropriate verb – *collect*, *bring* or *take* – in the correct form.

EXAMPLE: When you get to the airport, *take* the special bus that goes to the city centre.

1 I have to stop at the bookshop to .... a book I ordered.

2 When you come to stay with us in the country, don't forget to .... a pair of strong walking shoes.

3 Have you .... the tickets for the concert yet?

4 John .... Sarah to see her grandmother in hospital.

5 Everyone who came to our party .... something to eat and drink.

6 Could you please .... these flowers to Mrs Smith in Ward 14?

7 All patients should .... the medicine they have been prescribed.

8 Travellers on the coach trip may .... only one bag onto the bus.

9 John couldn't show me the holiday photos because he had forgotten to .... them with him.

10 We have a dozen volunteers in the town .... money to help the refugees.

3 Complete the sentences with *still*, *yet* or *already*.

EXAMPLES: I have been thinking about the problem for days but I *still* haven't found the answer.
Julia isn't here *yet* so we can't start the meeting.
I have *already* seen this film so I don't want to see it again.

1 I .... haven't had an answer to my letter.

2 John doesn't know if he has got the job ....

3 Jack is .... hoping to get a place at university.

4 Despite his age, Walter is .... very lively.

5 Madeleine has passed the exam but hasn't received her certificate ....

6 Before the runners got to the halfway point, they were .... exhausted.

7 We are .... hoping that the explorers will be found alive.

8 These books have .... not been returned to the library.

9 The garden is .... looking beautiful even though it isn't summer ....

10 Mr Ford has .... recovered from his illness.

11 I'm surprised you have finished .... Everybody else is .... working.

12 Most of the staff have .... found new jobs.

4 Complete the sentences with the correct preposition.

EXAMPLE: Mrs Faraday is very proud *of* her son Michael.

1 Nobody is enthusiastic .... the new training scheme.

2 Rudolph used to be admired .... millions of fans.

3 We are all very sad .... these unfortunate events.

4 The president is opposed .... these new proposals.

5 The principal was not aware .... what had happened.

6 Steven is not at all ashamed .... his actions.

7 Erica doesn't have a job and is dependent .... her parents.

8 The police were suspicious .... the four men in the car.

9 Ruth was found not guilty .... murder.

10 Janet was delighted .... her new dress.

71

unit **17** A SENSE OF ACHIEVEMENT

5 Read the text below and think of the word which best fits each space. Use only one word in each space. There is an example at the beginning (0).

14-Year-Old Seeks to Scale Everest

Mountaineers talk about (0) __how__ the trek up Everest separates the men from the boys. Fourteen-year-old Mark Pfetzer doesn't plan to be left (1) _____. 'It does scare me sometimes, (2) _____ I think about it, but I know I'll be safe,' said Mark, (3) _____ is training to be the youngest person to scale the world's highest peak. 'You don't take (4) _____ chances.'

More than 375 climbers have reached Everest's 8,853 metre summit (5) _____ Sir Edmund Hillary and Tensing Norkay scaled it in 1953, but 109 have died (6) _____ the attempt. The first man to stand on top of Everest says the boy might be (7) _____ off staying at home. 'I hope his parents are happy with (8) _____ he's trying to do and that he (9) _____ back alive,' Hillary said from his New Zealand home. 'I personally think if I were his parents I (10) _____ think it was an unwise thing to do.' Kenneth and Christine Pfetzer say they support (11) _____ son. 'I feel I can't refuse him, because it's the chance of a lifetime. If I ask him to put it (12) _____ he could lose that chance to be the youngest to (13) _____ his mark on the world,' Mrs Pfetzer said. Hillary isn't impressed. 'Nowadays, people think up (14) _____ kinds of gimmicky ideas to become the first or the youngest or the oldest. The media (15) _____ love it but the mountaineering world will laugh.'

6 Read the text below and look carefully at each line. Some of the lines are correct and some have a word which should not be there. Write the wrong word in the space provided and tick the correct lines. There are two examples at the beginning (0) and (00).

Winning a prize

I have got some very good news to tell you. You will be	0	✓
very suprised when you will hear it. I've just won a prize	00	will
of £500! The cheque has already arrived. The postman	1	
delivered it first this morning. I have never received a cheque	2	
for such a large amount as before and I really don't know how	3	
I'm going to spend with the money. Perhaps you can give me	4	
some ideas! You are probably wondering what I got the money	5	
for. Well, I wasn't lucky in the lottery, if that is it what you	6	
are thinking. I had to do something to get me the prize. In	7	
fact, I wrote a short story for a competition for the new writers	8	
that was advertised in a newspaper. I decided to have a go.	9	
It was a hard work writing the story but I managed to do it	10	
and, amazingly, I won first prize. I could hardly believe it, really.	11	
The most difficult thing which was thinking of a good ending. It	12	
took me a long time for to get it right but in the end I succeeded	13	
doing. My story will be published in the newspaper next week	14	
and I will be send a copy of it to you then.	15	

unit 18
TIME AFTER TIME

1 You are going to read a newspaper article about Jules Verne. For questions 1–8, choose the answer (A, B, C or D) which you think fits best according to the text.

Jules Verne's Dark Vision of Modern Life

PARIS – HORSE-DRAWN carriages clattered on the streets outside Jules Verne's Paris apartment, but it was quiet inside. There was no telephone and no radio – they had yet to be invented. The year was 1863. Soldiers were fighting the Civil War across the Atlantic. Workers were digging London's first underground railway line. And in Paris, the man who would become the best-selling French author of all time was imagining a bleak future. The only thing Verne could not have predicted was that a book he had written, rejected by his publisher, would wait 131 years until 1994, to be published.

The book's hero lived nearly a century in the future, in the year 1960. Technology and automation had supplanted the culture of the 1800s. Elevators whisked people up and down buildings. Trains took them back and forth from the suburbs. Neon lights, unknown in 1863, illuminated Verne's avenues. Concerts were performed in 10,000-seat auditoriums by single artists using electric amplifiers. 'Of the innumerable cars that passed in the paved roads, most moved without horses,' he wrote, 25 years before the first prototype of an automobile was built. 'They are propelled by an invisible force, the force of 20 or 30 horses by means of a motor run by gas combustion.' Verne's heroes, though, 'No longer stood in admiration of these marvels. They quietly took advantage of them, without being any happier, because of their speeded pace. One could feel the devil of money pushing them forward non-stop and without mercy.'

When Verne's editor read the manuscript he was not impressed. 'My dear Verne,' he wrote, 'You have undertaken an impossible task – as do all those like you who can see the future. But you have not succeeded. I wasn't waiting for something perfect, but I was waiting for something better. I would consider it a disaster for your name to be associated with this work. It is 100 steps below *Five Weeks in a Balloon*,' he said, referring to Verne's first success, which had appeared the same year. 'If you wait a year, you will agree with me. It is a little story and on a subject that isn't happy.' With that rebuff, the respectful author locked the manuscript and its dark vision of the future in a safe.

The safe remained in Verne's family after his death. Remarkably, no one tried to find the manuscript though it was officially listed at his death as being among his unpublished works. But the author's great-grandson remembered well that safe. 'It was an obsession of my childhood. I spent many long afternoons trying to open it. I tried all the keys of the house and others that fell into my hands. It represented for me an unsolvable mystery.' Finally, in 1989, using a blowtorch, he opened the safe. Inside were a few Russian bonds, an unfinished play and the unedited manuscript entitled *Paris in the Twentieth Century*. The manuscript's authenticity was verified by experts, and the 218-page book was published in France, drawing admiring reviews.

Nevertheless, this sad and nightmarish vision of the twentieth century came as a shock to many readers. For all the technical wonders Verne imagined, and largely because of them, Verne's Paris of 1960 is a forbidding place. Pollution is as thick as the London fog used to be, the countryside has disappeared, traffic jams clog the streets, tall buildings spoil the Parisian sky and offices are protected by security alarms.

Simone Verne, a literature professor, argues that the author's great gift was not in telling the future, but in following scientific advances through to a logical conclusion. 'The lost novel shows clearly that Verne's genius was not to have anticipated technological progress, but to foresee its troubling consequences for human beings. Now that we have walked on the moon and surpassed most of his inventions, it's time to take this into account. The world where money and technology rule is not, as we know, the best of all worlds.'

74

unit **18** TIME AFTER TIME

1. At the time Jules Verne was writing *Paris in the Twentieth Century*
   A the technology he described did not yet exist.
   B he wanted to write using advanced technology.
   C other writers were not as worried about the future as he was.
   D there was much concern about advances in military arms.

2. 'bleak' (line 14) means
   A happy
   B productive
   C unpleasant
   D unlikely

3. Jules Verne imagined a society where
   A people cared about other people.
   B artists were appreciated.
   C money was the most important thing.
   D people were excited by technology.

4. When Jules Verne's editor received the manuscript, he felt
   A the public was not ready for such originality.
   B the story-line needed changing.
   C disappointed with what he read.
   D Verne had lost his ability to tell a story.

5. How did Jules Verne react to the way his manuscript was received?
   A He was put off writing completely.
   B He attempted to make changes to the book.
   C He stopped writing books about the future.
   D He accepted the editor's judgement.

6. 'rebuff' (line 65) means
   A apology
   B rejection
   C request
   D complaint

7. How did the manuscript finally get published?
   A There was a revival of interest when Jules Verne died.
   B A family member found it by chance.
   C Literary experts suggested searching for it.
   D The family was getting rid of things it did not want.

8. What reaction was there when the manuscript was published?
   A The book was what everyone had expected.
   B Interest was limited to experts.
   C People found it funny to read.
   D People were surprised at how accurate Verne was.

2 Put the verb in the correct form – gerund or infinitive.

1. The farmer warned us .... (not enter) the field.

2. 'I don't remember ever .... (sign) this document,' said the chairman.

3. If you walk in these mountains, you risk .... (get) lost.

4. Tom always remembered .... (pick up) his briefcase before he left for work.

5. Jack suggested .... (buy) a new car.

6. Everyone tried .... (lift) the box but it didn't move at all.

7. We tried .... (grow) a new type of tomato but very few were edible.

8. Walter has not stopped .... (drive) even though he is 92.

9. Harriet used .... (live) in a small village when she was a child.

10. Don't forget .... (lock) the windows before you leave the house.

11. The children were not used to .... (study) so hard.

12. Martin finished .... (dig) the garden and then went into the house.

13. We regret .... (inform) you that we have no vacancies at the present time.

The Time Traveller

With this letter you will find a paperback book. It is as your	0 ..... as .....
birthday present and I hope you enjoy reading it. It is called	00 ..... ✓ .....
The Time Machine by H.G. Wells and it was first published	1 .....
in year 1895, but the English is quite easy to understand and it	2 .....
is a short book, only about 100 pages total. It is	3 .....
about a man who builds a time machine on which he travels to	4 .....
the year of 8271 where he finds one group of people living	5 .....
on the surface and another living underground. The Morlocks,	6 .....
who live underground, steal away his time machine, making it	7 .....
impossible for him to return back to his own time. He has a	8 .....
lot of exciting adventures before he eventually gains the control	9 .....
of his machine again. I don't want you to give too much of	10 .....
the story away, or you won't find it exciting to be read. I	11 .....
think you will be really impressed by the part in which he	12 .....
travels 30 million years into the future and is being attacked	13 .....
by those giant crabs! The ending is very mysterious and I	14 .....
won't reveal it. Do let me know if you enjoyed this story.	15 .....

4 Complete the second sentence so that it has a similar meaning to the first sentence. Use the word given and other words to complete each sentence. You must use between two and five words. Do not change the word given.

1. Promise never to see me again and I will return the ring.
   condition
   I will return the ring .... never to see me again.

2. The boxer didn't even try to defend himself.
   made
   The boxer .... to defend himself.

3. What did you tell the gardener to do?
   instructions
   What .... the gardener?

4. Charlotte started laughing before I finished the story.
   got
   Before I .... the story, Charlotte started laughing.

5. 'I did not sign that document,' said the accountant.
   denied
   The accountant .... that document.

6. Do you think it would have been a good idea to buy tickets in advance?
   should
   Do you think .... tickets in advance?

7. It's true that Frank was once in prison, isn't it?
   to
   Frank ...., hasn't he?

8. I think the witness was mistaken about my client's identity.
   for
   In my opinion, the witness .... else.

9. It's tomorrow that Jack arrives, isn't it?
   will
   Jack ...., ... he?

10. It is rumoured that they are going to get married.
    a
    There .... that they are going to get married.

5 Complete the sentences with a phrasal verb based on *fall*.

EXAMPLE: If you don't look after your teeth, one day they will all ..*fall out*..

1. My son is learning to walk but he keeps ....

2. John was badly shaken when he .... his bike.

3. The comedian was so amusing that he had everyone ....

4. I'm happy to .... with other people's plans.

5. Harry and Sally .... when they had an argument about who should pay the bill.

6. The excellent sales of the product began to .... when a rival appeared on the market.

7. The jockey .... the horse at the first fence.

8. Our holiday plans have .... so we're going to have to think of somewhere else to go.

unit 19
EXPLORATION, ADVENTURE, INVENTION

1 You are going to read a magazine article about an accident on a mountain. Five paragraphs have been removed from the article. Fill each gap (1–5) with the paragraph which you think fits best from the list A–F. There is one paragraph which you do not need to use.

TAKING ON THE OGRE

The mountains of Britain and the rest of Europe are by now well travelled. Almost every ridge and face has been climbed. It's rare to be on a mountain alone, and the quality of the rescue services means that an injured climber can be whisked to hospital in a helicopter in a matter of minutes.

1

On 12 July 1977 the British Mountaineer Doug Scott reached the summit of The Ogre in Pakistan's Karakoram. The 7283-metre peak had tested both Scott and his partner Chris Bonington like almost no other with very difficult climbing all the way to the top. It was a great first attempt but it was now late in the day, and neither had sleeping bags in which to spend the night, which made a quick descent imperative if they were to survive.

2

Bonington lowered himself down to reach his injured partner, carefully avoiding Scott's mistake, and the two men spent a miserable night trying to keep warm in the freezing temperatures.

3

Then the storm broke and the team were trapped for two days with no food. On the third day, even though the blizzard still raged outside, they set off again before they lost their remaining strength.

4

But their ordeal was far from over: when lowering himself down, Bonington came off the end of the rope, fell and broke two ribs, later contracting pneumonia. The retreat became even more desperate as a result.

5

Even then Scott wasn't safe. The team made a stretcher out of wooden poles and a team of local Balti porters carried him almost to the village of Askole where a helicopter was waiting. On approach to the town of Skardu, however, the engine failed and the helicopter crash-landed, fortunately with no casualties. Bonington had to wait seven more days at Askole before evacuation.

A Scott knew that his chances were very slim. They had first to climb back over another, lower, summit and then descend thousands of feet of very difficult ground. On the way back to their highest camp, a snow cave dug into the ridge, they met two other members of the team, Mo Anthoine and Clive Rowland, who dug big steps for Scott to crawl along, and eventually they all reached the shelter.

B Eight days after breaking both his ankles on top of one of the hardest mountains in the world, Doug Scott crawled into their base camp at 10.30 p.m. to discover it abandoned. Thinking that the team were all dead, the remaining team had dismantled it. Mo Anthoine had to chase after them to tell them to return with medicines and food.

C In the greater ranges rescue is a different matter. Long approaches to lonely valleys, in areas where the infrastructure is basic, mean that if something goes seriously wrong, you're probably on your own. It certainly adds a great deal to the psychological pressure of climbing a mountain if you know that a broken ankle can kill you. Accidents happen to the best of climbers.

D If they had been tied together, he would never have reached the summit. They would jointly have been forced to retreat, but both might have survived. However, these traditional bonds are now widely ignored in Himalayan mountaineering. Above 8000 metres many climb alone. At that height, they say, a partner could not rescue you without risking death.

E Clive Rowland led the way over the west summit and they started descending once more. Scott wore out the knees of five pairs of over-trousers during his fight for survival.

F Scott started to lower himself down from the summit, and spotted some pitons hammered into the rock to one side. Bracing his feet against the rock, he eased his way across towards them, but the falling temperature had frozen the water covering the slabs. As he lost his footing, he swung wildly back across the wall. Raising his feet to absorb the impact, he slammed into a wall, breaking both legs just above the ankle.

2 Read the text below. Use the word given in capitals at the end of each line to form a word that fits in the space in the same line. There is an example at the beginning (0).

Danger in the mountains

In mountainous areas, such as the Alps, (0) ___electrical___ storms	**ELECTRIC**
can be terrifying experiences both for (1) _____ and local inhabitants.	**MOUNTAIN**
Climbers describe (2) _____ incidents in which their hair stands on	**FRIGHT**
end, they hear buzzing noises, see flashes and feel (3) _____ in the	**DEFENCE**
face of powerful (4) _____ forces beyond their control. There is	**NATURE**
no (5) _____ against lightning bolts, which nearly always cause	**PROTECT**
death, usually from heart (6) _____ but precautions can be taken.	**FAIL**
Climbers who are (7) _____ carry their ice-axes low down because	**CARE**
if they are (8) _____ high up they attract lightning. It is important to	**HOLD**
have a good (9) _____ of weather conditions. When anvil-shaped	**KNOW**
clouds are seen, it is an (10) _____ that lightning may soon strike.	**INDICATE**

unit **19** EXPLORATION, ADVENTURE, INVENTION

3 Read the text below and decide which answer (A, B, C or D) best fits each space. The exercise begins with an example (0).

Inside the volcano

One of the most dangerous tasks for geologists is the investigation of (0) .... volcanoes. Several geologists have (1) .... their lives while making scientific observations of volcanoes which are in the (2) .... of erupting. Scientists can make important (3) .... by studying the behaviour of volcanoes, but dangerous situations can occur (4) .... Even if lava is not actually (5) .... , there may be rockfalls, the surface may (6) .... without warning and there may be pockets of poisonous gas. Despite the dangers, the work must be done because knowing more about how and why volcanoes erupt will help scientists to (7) .... accurate forecasts. They can then (8) .... reliable warnings that will help to (9) .... lives and avoid damage to property.

Recently, robots have been invented which can do much of the work previously done by humans. In fact, they can do more. One robot spent seven days (10) .... in the crater of a volcano in Alaska where no human could have survived. This robot looked like a spider, with eight legs for (11) .... on steep and uneven surfaces. Unfortunately, it had to be rescued by humans after it had fallen over on (12) .... mud. Scientists do not (13) .... the robot as a failure because its cameras and other instruments (14) .... valuable information during the seven days that it was in (15) ....

0	A	active	B	live	C	animated	D	vital
1	A	lost	B	taken	C	quit	D	passed
2	A	period	B	process	C	time	D	season
3	A	findings	B	data	C	discoveries	D	enquiries
4	A	unexpectedly	B	suprisingly	C	quickly	D	unluckily
5	A	rolling	B	pouring	C	moving	D	flowing
6	A	give through	B	give out	C	give up	D	give way
7	A	have	B	make	C	say	D	predict
8	A	give	B	announce	C	guarantee	D	state
9	A	secure	B	save	C	maintain	D	rescue
10	A	alone	B	isolated	C	deep	D	far
11	A	stability	B	strength	C	power	D	flexibility
12	A	dangerous	B	sticky	C	greasy	D	slippery
13	A	take	B	conclude	C	regard	D	accept
14	A	recorded	B	took	C	observed	D	found
15	A	work	B	movement	C	location	D	operation

unit 19 EXPLORATION, ADVENTURE, INVENTION

4 Complete the second sentence so that it has a similar meaning to the first sentence. Use the word given and other words to complete each sentence. You must use between two and five words. Do not change the word given.

1 Let's go and see what's happening over there!
look
Shall we go and .... what's happening over there?

2 If only I had enough money to buy that ring!
afford
I .... that ring.

3 'Faster! Faster!' shouted our coach.
move
'Get .... !' shouted our coach.

4 If you listen to your car radio, you can keep away from traffic jams.
stuck
You can .... traffic jams by listening to your car radio.

5 I would never apply for such a job.
consider
I would never .... for such a job.

6 Nobody knows what Professor Smith's letter means.
of
The .... Professor Smith's letter is not clear to anybody.

7 There is a strong possibility of snow tomorrow.
as
It looks .... tomorrow.

8 Emma is the one who has to make the decision.
up
It's .... decide.

9 I'm too tired to finish this work today.
so
I'm .... finish this work today.

10 The explorers' food supplies were almost finished.
hardly
The explorers .... food left.

5 Complete the sentences with the appropriate word – *fault*, *blame* or *mistake* – in the correct form.

EXAMPLE: It's not my ___fault___ that you didn't finish your work.

1 The police are trying to decide who was to .... for the accident.

2 There was a .... on the film and none of the photographs came out.

3 John has many qualities and few ....

4 It was a .... for us to have a holiday on the coast in the winter.

5 Martha .... her father for the fact that she had not been able to decide her own career.

6 Whose .... was it that the pot got broken?

7 It's impossible to learn without making ....

8 The manufacturers have recalled all models of this washing machine as there is a serious .... which must be put right.

9 It's impossible to know who to .... for the collapse of the building.

10 The child is too young to be .... for what he did.

81

unit 20 CONTRASTS

1 You are going to read an article from a newspaper. For questions 1–8, choose the answer (A, B, C or D) which you think fits best according to the text.

The man who lived to tell tales

Ron Jones has reinvented himself. In the 1980s, he was a computer expert with a vast salary. Now he has become a house-husband, staying at home to look after his baby son while his wife, Debbie, works. In between nappy changes and bottle feeds, he has produced the novel he has always wished to write. What is the reason for his transformation? On 12 December 1988, Ron Jones was aboard the 7.08 a.m. train from Southampton to London when it collided with another train at Clapham Junction, killing 36 passengers. He survived with minor injuries, but the emotional aftermath changed his life into a nightmare. Now he has awoken. At 47, he has become the author Alex Keegan: his first novel, *Cuckoo*, was published this month.

Born and brought up in South Wales, Keegan says he 'had the classic deprived childhood. There was my mother, father, two older sisters and me living in one room.' His parents split up and he spent almost two years in a children's home, and was then sent to foster parents. He left school at fifteen, then joined the Royal Air Force. There was a short-lived marriage, with two children and numerous jobs. Keegan then went to Liverpool University to study psychology, and had another brief marriage. By the mid-eighties he had set himself up in Southampton as a computer consultant, training staff for companies with his then girlfriend, Clare.

While commuting back and forth to London to work for a City firm, he came to know a few of the regulars on the 7.08 train. On the day of the accident he was late and could not get his usual seat in the buffet, so he sat in a carriage further towards the rear of the train. He was dozing as the train approached London. 'There was an almighty bang. At first I thought I'd been in a fight. The guy opposite had just been thrown into me. I looked up and saw that the roof of the carriage had split.' He escaped with cuts and bruises, but the emotional effects ran deeper. He had been in the fourth carriage back: he discovered that the commuters he usually sat with had been killed. 'People told me I was very lucky, but I just felt I was in the wrong place. One minute you think you're the centre of the universe, then something like that makes you realise you're not. Afterwards, I was just a mess. Back at work, I found I couldn't concentrate. I'd start a sentence and forget what I was talking about. It caused a lot of stress between me and my girlfriend. She was watching the business collapsing around our ears and I just didn't care. In that situation, the problem is that you look more or less the same. But your inner motivation, your drive and concentration are gone.'

His girlfriend left, and Jones hit rock bottom. 'I was on my own. I hadn't paid the mortgage for a year and I had no way of ever getting back.' Gradually he pulled himself out of it. He met his current wife in 1990. When she became pregnant, they agreed that he would stay at home and be house-husband when the baby arrived. 'I was really frightened of trying to do another big-earning job,' he explains. 'I didn't believe I would be able to hold down a job again. It would have to be something else, but I had no idea what.' He turned his hand to writing, and with the birth of his son in October 1992, he set about completing his first novel. 'Alex would wake up. I'd feed him. In the early days he'd be quite happy playing on the floor while I sat and wrote 500 words. It was great. Sometimes I would type with him sitting on my lap.'

Late last year Ron Jones metamorphosed fully into Alex Keegan. He signed a three-book deal and in February his agent sold the television rights to *Cuckoo*. While he admits that, financially, things are still difficult he has no regrets. 'What happened at Clapham changed my life. If I was going up and down to London, I might be on £80,000 a year, but I'd hardly see the children. Now I can take a two-minute break and have a cuddle. It's wonderful.'

1   What has Ron Jones now achieved?
    A He has become a father for the first time.
    B He has been able to give up a job he disliked.
    C He has developed a new way of living.
    D He has plenty of money to spend.

2   What does he think about his childhood?
    A It was difficult to get on with his parents.
    B It led to emotional problems.
    C It helped him to develop a positive outlook.
    D It was a hard way to begin life.

3   When the accident happened, he
    A was sitting in his usual place.
    B was not travelling on his usual train.
    C had changed places with someone else.
    D was in an unfamiliar part of the train.

4   How did he feel about the accident?
    A His physical injuries distressed him.
    B He was relieved not to be killed.
    C He was disturbed by his good fortune.
    D His worries were about his friends.

5   What effect did the accident have?
    A He began to criticise his girlfriend's work.
    B He could not concentrate on business.
    C He paid great attention to work.
    D He decided he wanted to change his job.

6   'that' (line 46) refers to
    A the centre of the universe
    B the accident
    C the wrong place
    D the train

7   Alex agreed to be a house-husband because
    A he wanted time to write.
    B he was determined to get to know his son.
    C he was frightened of the idea of travelling.
    D he feared the demands a job would make.

8   Thinking about his life today, Alex
    A believes more money would solve his problems.
    B regrets the experience of Clapham.
    C wishes he had moved to London.
    D enjoys the life he leads.

2 Complete the sentences with the correct word – *over, in, as, until, while, before, on, at*.

1 Jack was astonished that his interview had lasted .... two hours.

2 I waited .... the last train had arrived and then left the station.

3 The football match started exactly .... time.

4 Drive faster or we won't get to the airport .... time to do some shopping.

5 The police arrived .... exactly the right moment.

6 There are no more flights .... 6 a.m. tomorrow.

7 I waited .... everyone had gone before tidying up.

8 Someone stole Bernard's briefcase .... he realised what was happening.

9 John became interested in sumo wrestling .... he was studying in Japan.

10 The photographer took the picture exactly .... the prince fell off his horse.

3 Put the verb in the correct form – gerund or infinitive.

1 We all objected to .... (delay) for so long.

2 I always try to avoid .... (drive) through the centre of town.

3 I advise you .... (not tell) him the truth.

4 We started our journey at dawn and stopped .... (eat) at 9 a.m.

5 Do you regret .... (not warn) them in time?

6 Jack decided .... (buy) a house in the village.

7 'Forget .... (revise) for the exam! Go to the party!' said Mary.

unit **20** CONTRASTS

4 Read the text below and think of the word which best fits each space. Use only one word in each space. There is an example at the beginning (0).

Swimmer is fed up with marathon swim

A swimmer trying to swim (0) ....across.... the Atlantic said that he was getting fed up after more than two weeks in the water and (1) .... it hard to sleep. 'There's a certain disappointment, (2) .... suffering,' Guy Delage, 42, said in a radio interview (3) .... the Atlantic. He is about 1,100 km into his trip, (4) .... stretches from the Cape Verde Islands (5) .... Africa to the Caribbean island of Martinique. 'My dream has lasted eight years, and now it's gradually (6) .... replaced by a reality that isn't exactly (7) .... I had dreamt of.'

Delage has spent eighteen days (8) .... sea in his bid for the first trans-Atlantic swim and (9) .... about 2,800 kilometres to go, braving sharks, storms and loneliness. He spends about ten hours a day in the water and the (10) .... drifting westward on ocean currents on a small wind-powered raft. It follows him (11) .... he swims by a satellite tracking device. But Delage said the noise of the small windmills (12) .... the raft bother (13) .... 'It's very difficult to sleep at night,' he said. 'The raft is so uncomfortable that it's a (14) .... of relief to get into the water.'

Delage has raced sailing yachts and piloted ultralight solo aircraft. In 1991, he flew an ultralight plane of his (15) .... design across the Atlantic in 26 hours.

5 Read the text below. Use the word given in capitals at the end of each line to form a word that fits in the space in the same line. There is an example at the beginning (0).

Komodo Dragons

The komodo dragon, or to give its (0) ....scientific.... name — **SCIENCE**

Varanus komodoensis is a giant lizard that grows to a (1) .... — **LONG**

of 3 metres and has an average (2) .... of 136 kilograms. They — **WEIGH**

are (3) .... on the Indonesian island of Komodo, after which — **FIND**

they are named, and a few (4) .... islands. Komodo dragons — **NEIGHBOUR**

(5) .... on deer and other small mammals. The young can climb — **FOOD**

trees although fully-grown dragons do not have this (6) .... All — **ABLE**

dragons are good (7) .... Because of their size and speed, they — **SWIM**

can be (8) .... to human beings. Despite this, they are a popular — **DANGER**

tourist attraction because of their (9) .... to dinosaurs. However, — **RESEMBLE**

they are not (10) .... of dinosaurs. Dragons are now a protected — **RELATE**

species because their numbers are quite small.